CONTEMPORARY ECONOMIC PERSPECTIVES IN EDUCATION

Contemporary Economic Perspectives in Education

Edited by Kristof De Witte

Leuven University Press

© 2015 Leuven University Press / Presses Universitaires de Louvain / Universitaire Pers Leuven, Minderbroedersstraat 4, B-3000 Leuven/Louvain (Belgium)

All rights reserved. Except in those cases expressly determined by law, no part of this publication may be multiplied, saved in an automated data file or made public in any way whatsoever without the express prior written consent of the publishers.

ISBN 978 94 6270 025 3
D / 2015 / 1869 / 3
NUR: 780, 840

Cover design & layout: Friedemann Vervoort,
Coverimage: shutterstock

Table of Contents

Introduction

Chapter 1:
Systematic Reviews in Education Research: When Do Effect Studies Provide Evidence?

1. Introduction	11
2. First order conditions	13
3. Second order conditions	19
4. Third order conditions	21
5. Applying the inclusion criteria in practice	22
6. Concluding remarks	26
Appendix A. Inclusion criteria used in review articles in the Review of Education, edition 2010	30

Chapter 2:
Selection Bias in Educational Issues and the Use of Heckman's Sample Selection Model

1. Introduction	35
2. Selection bias and causality	35
3. Heckman's sample selection model	42
4. The sample selection model in educational research	44
5. Conclusion	49

Chapter 3:
The Causal Effect of Single-Sex Education versus Coeducation on Motivation and Educational Attainments. Evidence from a Randomized Experiment in Secondary Education

1. Introduction	53
2. Literature review	56
3. Flemish education system	61
4. Data and experiment	62
5. Quantitative analysis	64
6. Qualitative analysis	69
7. Conclusion and policy recommendations	71

Chapter 4:
Benchmarking and Operational Management: an Application of Frontier Analysis to Dutch Secondary Education

1. Introduction	77
2. Methodology	77
3. Data	78
4. Results	82
5. Conclusions	87

Chapter 5:
Schools' Efficiency and Equity: Evidence from a Stochastic Frontier Approach with Translog Specification

1. Introduction	89
2. Methodology and data	90
3. Results and discussion	91
Appendix A	97

Chapter 6: Do Nurses React to Inter-Industry Wage Differentials? – Evidence of Nursing Graduates in the Netherlands

1. Introduction	99
2. Wage differentials and job-related skills in the literature	100
3. The life sciences and health industry in the Netherlands	102
4. Conceptual framework	103
5. Empirical strategy	104
6. Data	108
7. Descriptive statistics	110
8. Results	113
9. Discussion and conclusions	118

Short Author Bios of the Corresponding Authors   123

Introduction

Education accounts for 13% of total public spending in the average OECD country (OECD, 2013). Moreover, as resources devoted to education grow faster than the total public expenditures in the period 1995 - 2005, education becomes increasingly important during recent years. The latest economic crisis did not change this pattern.

Simultaneously with the increasing share in public resources, there is an increasing availability of standardized educational outcome variables. The OECD takes a lead with standardized outcomes at age 15 (Programme for International Student Assessment - PISA data). The International Association for the Evaluation of Educational Achievement (IEA) developed a standardized test for mathematics and science studies (Trends in International Mathematics and Science Study - TIMSS data) and for literacy (Progress in International Reading Literacy Study - PIRLS data). The international comparisons are heavily debated among policy makers and civil servants. For some education systems, e.g. the Flemish region of Belgium, the steady decline in performance on those rankings is even explicitly mentioned as a reason for large reforms of the educational system.

A final trend in educational policy is 'evidence based education'. This means that educational policy should be based on the best available evidence. In many countries 'evidence based education' marked the start of renewed interest to education research. For example in the Netherlands, the Educational Council published in 2006 an influential report on the need for evidence based education. It stated that there are too many innovations in education, while there is little information on 'what works'. Evidence based education aims to estimate in a causal way what works and what does not work. To bridge the gap between science, policy makers and schools, the 'Best Evidence Encyclopedia' has been developed (www.bestevidence.nl / www.bestevidence.org). This website provides an overview of evidence on various interventions in primary, secondary and higher education.

Economists are well placed to study education. They are intrinsically interested in spending. They want to examine whether resources are spent in an effective (i.e., doing the right things) and efficient (i.e., doing the things right) way. By focusing on educational efficiency, economists can provide intuitive insights to obtain more value for money. Moreover, the effectiveness concerns are related to the 'evidence based education' idea. In contrasts to other disciplines, economists examine educational issues with a different methodological toolbox. For example, to obtain causal inference, they compare a treatment group with a control group. In education, this corresponds to some students who are randomly assigned to a treated group, and who are compared to students without a treatment. While non-economists point to ethical issues of a similar randomization of students, economists rigorously argue that without proper evidence of the effect of the treatment, none of the students receives an advantage. Only if the evidence shows that the treatment is beneficial (and cost-effective), the treatment can be generalized to a broader group of students.

While experimental evidence has the advantage of a high internal validity (i.e., it measures the effect of the treatment precisely), it suffers from a rather low external validity (i.e., the outcomes only apply for a selected population). An interesting approach to deal with this issue is by mimicking an experiment. A similar technique is called matching: it matches treated students to students without a treatment. By matching on all observed characteristics, the idea is that also on the unobserved characteristics the students in the treated and control group will be similar.

Both methodologies allow economists to avoid 'endogeneity' issues. In case of endogeneity there is a correlation between the variable of interest and the error term in the regression. This correlation makes that the estimated results are biased. There are many sources of endogeneity, from which we discuss three. First there is selection bias. This indicates that the evaluated observations can choose to be treated. In this case of selection, one will obtain biased inference as only the most motivated observations will participate. An experiment, for example, avoids this selection bias as the research randomly assigns observations to a treatment and control group. A second reason for endogeneity arises from unobserved heterogeneity, or omitted variables. This is the case if a third, often unobserved variable, correlates with the variable of interest. For example, if education of the parents make that students are self-selected in particular groups. Finally, reversed causality refers to the direction of cause-and-effect. Too often, economists argue that the direction of the effect is the opposite of what is generally believed.

This book contributes to this growing field of 'education economics'. The first chapter provides a detailed approach on how economists treat earlier evidence. It uses the case of systematic reviews to show how studies are often based on rather *ad hoc* inclusion criteria that may lead to inconsistencies in the outcomes generated. This chapter therefore derives a set of inclusion criteria from the theoretical literature on causal inference. It, furthermore, presents a list of study characteristics that reviews should minimally provide (if possible). By comparing the derived inclusion criteria in this study with the inclusion criteria used in several educational reviews, the first chapter concludes that the generated outcomes of systematic reviews frequently rely on rather incomplete and inconsistent inclusion criteria.

A second chapter is more econometric in nature (i.e., it combines economics with mathematics and statistics) and points to the first source of endogeneity: selection bias. Selection bias arises in non-random samples when unobserved factors are both correlated with the probability of being selected in the sample and with the dependent variable of interest. A common identification strategy when selection bias is suspected, is to apply the 'heckit model' proposed by Noble Prize Winner James Heckman, who reconceptualized selection bias as a form of omitted variable bias that can be corrected by adding a control to the model that reflects the probability of selection into the sample. This chapter provides an introduction to the use of heckit models in the field of educational issues. It discusses the importance of selection bias in educational research, reviews the use of the heckit model in the educational literature and presents an overview of the extent to which heckit models re-adjust previous findings. The strengths and weaknesses of the heckit approach are critically assessed, research gaps are identified and potential directions for future research are explored.

A third chapter provides an example of experimental evidence on a topic of high policy relevance. About all OECD tests like PISA, TIMSS and PIRLS rigorously show that boys are underperforming girls. This chapter summarizes some didactical tools at school and course level to reduce the underperformance of boys. One suggested route to avoid this underperformance is by making single-sex classes, again. However, the literature lacks sound evidence on the effects of single-sex education. This third chapter examines the effect of single-sex education versus coeducation on student's motivation and educational attainments. To estimate the impact of boys-only, girls-only and mixed-sex education, it runs an experiment in a large Flemish school. By randomizing 12 to 14 years old students to homogenous and heterogeneous gender groups, it observes in a quantitative analysis that the gender composition significantly influences the motivation of students. In comparison to the coeducation groups, the single-sex groups experience a significantly lower motivation for the courses. There are, however, age differences. Younger students like better coeducation than older students. Chapter 3 does not find significant differences in educational attainments due to coeducation. Only for the 12-13 years old, the girls-only group significantly outperforms the boys-only group. To open the black box of the quantitative analysis, the experiment also involves a qualitative analysis. It confirms the quantitative results and indicates that class dynamics play an important role in the effect of coeducation.

While Chapter 3 focusses on the effectiveness of educational innovations, Chapter 4 and 5 focus on the efficiency of education provision. Using evidence from two different countries, the Netherlands and Italy respectively, they show how economists can provide policy makers concrete tools to reduce costs for a given level of education outcomes. Chapter 4 makes the explicit link between cost-efficiency, economies of scale and autonomous productivity. The latter is derived from the year-on-year changes in costs, after they have been adjusted for changes in production, prices of resources used and operational management of individual institutions.

Chapter 5 combines efficiency with equity of education. The economic theory suggests that there can be trade-offs between efficiency and equity, to the extent that for improving the former dimension of a school's performance (i.e. the ability of "producing" higher achievement with the minimum level of resources) would require grouping/segregating students by ability or socioeconomic characteristics. Chapter 5 shows that this trade-off is not necessarily present.

A final chapter makes the bridge between education and the labour market. Policy makers do not only judge the efficiency and effectiveness of education on short term test scores at a given age (as in, e.g., PISA, TIMSS or PIRLS) but are mainly concerned with education as a mechanism to create prosperity and welfare in the long run. The formation of skills in higher vocational education matter for the earning potential later in life. Chapter 6 explores the extent to which inter-industry wage differentials can explain the decision of nursing graduates to quit the life sciences and health industry (LSH). Using the theoretical framework of Lazaer (2009), it is predicted that nurses drop-out of LSH in case their general skills pay-off more in foreign industries than seniority in LSH. It is also predicted that industries demanding rigorous specific skills are prone to skill shortages. The empirical strategy benefits from data of the Dutch higher vocational school leaving monitor on abilities necessary to perform in the job. Owing to iterative one-to-one matching, this chapter makes 2003 to 2011 graduates homogenous with respect to their general skills.

As a final note, we hope that the book shows that the economic perspective on education provides innovative and methodological sound insights to contemporary education issues as single-sex education, resource efficiency and labour market. This is exactly what the research center 'Leuven Economics of Education Research' (LEER – www.feb.kuleuven.be/leer) of Faculty of Economics and Business of the KU Leuven aims. Using multi-disciplinary insights from labour, education, industrial, managerial and public economics, LEER provides original and evidence based answers to important policy issues. While this book marks the start of this new research center, given the importance of education, we hope that this book will be the first in a long series.

Kristof De Witte
January 2015

CHAPTER 1

Systematic Reviews in Education Research: When Do Effect Studies Provide Evidence?[1]

Chris Van Klaveren[2], Inge De Wolf[3]

"Although purely descriptive research has an important role to play, often social science research is about cause and effect. A causal relationship is useful for making predictions about the consequences of changing circumstances or policies; it tells us what would happen in alternative (or counterfactual) worlds (Angrist and Pischke, 2009)"

1. Introduction

Systematic literature reviews summarize the results of previous studies to inform the reader on the *effectiveness* of certain programs and give structure to the findings of larger amounts of empirical studies that focus on the same research topic. By putting the emphasis on causality, these reviews recognize that policy makers and scientist should be informed about causal relationships to make (more) accurate predictions about the consequences of changing circumstances or policies (Angrist and Pischke, 2009). For this purpose a distinction is being made between studies that focus on causal inference and other studies (i.e. correlational studies). Biomedical and psychological reviews frequently define consistent and clearly stated a priori inclusion criteria to make this distinction (see for example Slavin, 1984; 1986; 2008, and What Works Clearinghouse, 2008).

Currently, there is no predefined set of inclusion criteria for writing a systematic review on causal inference in economic and social sciences in general. This has, first of all, to do with the fact that many evaluation approaches on causal inference were developed and applied in the last two decades (Imbens and Wooldridge, 2008). Examples are regression discontinuity, instrumental variable analysis, and matching approaches. These evaluation approaches are frequently used in economics and other educational sciences (see, for example, Ou and Reynolds, 2010, and Greene and Winters, 2007). Each of these evaluation methods have their own pros and cons, as is illustrated by numerous methodological reviews: Rubin (1974), Angrist and Kruger (1999), Webbink (2005), Blundell and Costa Dias (2009), Imbens and Wooldridge (2008), Angrist & Pischke (2009), Imbens (2009).

---

[1] We would like to thank Kristof De Witte, Hessel Oosterbeek, and Robert Slavin for their valuable remarks.
[2] The corresponding author is affiliated with TIER at Maastricht University and the Amsterdam School of Economics. Email: cp.vanklaveren@maastrichtuniversity.nl.
[3] The author is affiliated with Maastricht University (Academische Werkplaats Onderwijs) and University of Amsterdam (TIER). Email: i.dewolf@maastrichtuniversity.nl

Furthermore, there are few experiments in the economic and social science literature. Inclusion criteria in biomedical and psychological reviews are purely formulated with randomized controlled (field) experiments as a reference point, but these experiments are often not feasible in social sciences (see, for example, Cook, 2002, and Rodrik, 2008). The combination of the lack of randomized experiments and the larger variety in evaluation methods for causal effects, makes it more difficult to formulate consistent and transparent a priori inclusion criteria in economic reviews.

The inclusion criteria that are currently used in systematic economic reviews are not derived from the theoretical literature on causal inference. As a consequence, it is not clear how *complete* specific sets of inclusion criteria are, in the sense that it remains unclear if additional inclusion criteria should have been specified, or if the specified inclusion criteria are overly restrictive. In the former case, correlational studies may slip through the selection procedure imposing a bias on the review findings, and in the latter case, qualitative good and causal studies may not be considered in the review, which can also impose a bias on the research findings.

This study derives a set of inclusion criteria from the theoretical literature on causal inference and can be applied in systematic reviews to select and rate studies. By doing so, the underlying assumptions of the derived inclusion criteria are at all times clear. This study is complementary with currently existing biomedical and psychological studies that derive inclusion criteria from a fundamental discussion of theory (Slavin, 1984; 1986; 2008, and What Works Clearinghouse, 2008) because it (a) focuses on economic and other social sciences literature and (b) considers the econometric evaluation methods on causal mechanisms of the last two decades.

The second study contribution is that it presents study characteristics that reviews should minimally provide to the reader (if possible) in order to be informative. These study characteristics are also derived from the theoretical literature on causal inference and can be used, together with the derived inclusion criteria, to select and rate the results of empirical studies at its true evidence.

Thirdly, this study examines if systematic review outcomes rely on complete and consistent inclusion criteria. For this purpose we compare the derived inclusion criteria in this study to the inclusion criteria used in 18 review studies that were published in the Review of Education Research in 2010.

Finally, this study is of practical value for policy makers, principals and teachers, as it provides them with an easy-to-apply list of rules that can be used to review empirical studies for evidence based policy or evidence based practice.

The theoretical framework used to derive the inclusion criteria from is inspired by Imbens (2009), who refers in his paper to conditions related to research methodology (first order conditions) and conditions related to analytical and data issues (second order conditions). We, additionally, define a group of third order conditions, which are related to representativeness, impact and usefulness of an estimated causal relationship. These third order conditions enfold external validity, the relevance of effect sizes of estimators, and the extent to which experimental outcomes are informative for implementing an intervention in practice. Based on these first, second and third order conditions, this study concludes that there are (*only*) four rather objective inclusion criteria that systematic literature reviews should apply.

The methodological focus of this study results in inclusion criteria that are methodological as well. There are, however, also other relevant inclusion criteria for systematic reviews that are related to the nature of the evaluated intervention. Slavin (2008), for example, formulated a list of conditions that interventions must satisfy in order to be informative. One of these conditions is that evaluation studies should only be included in reviews if the duration of the evaluated intervention is minimally 12 weeks. This condition gives more certainty that the reviewed interventions have substantial impact and are of practical use in education (Slavin, 2008).

We proceed as follows. Sections 2 to 4 discuss the first, second and third order conditions. From these conditions we derive (a) minimum quality standards that should be used as inclusion criteria and (b) study characteristics that reviews should show in order to be informative. The study characteristics indicate if a particular study is relevant in the 'eye of the beholder', but are not related to the quality of the study, in the sense that it is not related to the internal validity of the estimated impact. Section 5 compares the derived inclusion criteria to the applied inclusion criteria by 18 review studies published in the Review of Education Research. Finally, Section 7, concludes the main findings.

2. First order conditions

A missing data problem is underlying each evaluation study, which is nicely illustrated by the potential outcome model, introduced by Neyman (1990), Roy (1951); Rubin (1974, 1976) and Holland (1986). The model recognizes that there are two potential outcomes for each person[4] to consider if we want to measure the effectiveness of an intervention. The intervention may represent a real intervention, such as a nation wide policy intervention or a summer school program, but it may also represent a characteristic, such as having a teacher credential. A person may either be subject to the intervention or may not, but no person can be in both states simultaneously. Since we never observe both potential outcomes at the same time it is not possible to measure the effect of the intervention directly. To the outcome not observed is generally referred to as the *counterfactual outcome*.

Given that there are always counterfactual outcomes in evaluation studies, the effectiveness of an intervention can only be measured if there is a control group to which the outcomes of the persons subject to the intervention (the intervention group) can be compared to. This control group and the intervention group should have (on average) similar observable and unobservable characteristics that influence the outcome variable, such that outcome differences between the two groups are due to the intervention alone. The effect of the intervention on the outcome variable is then obtained by comparing the outcomes of the intervention group with those of the control group. It follows that the degree to which studies are able to measure how the outcome variable is causally related to the intervention (i.e. deliver evidence) depends on how well these studies are able to construct a proper control group.

This section discusses the methodological conditions that are related to how well studies are able to construct a proper control group. Because these methodological conditions are unrelated to data problems or analytical problems, and therefore always

---

[4] Throughout the paper we conveniently refer to persons as the unit of analysis. Obviously the unit of analysis may also be countries, organizations, firms, classrooms, schools, teachers, employers etc.

apply, we refer to them as first order conditions. We can distinguish three types of studies that construct the control group in a fundamentally different way:

1. Randomized Controlled Trials.
2. Observational Studies:
    a. Quasi Experimental Studies,
    b. Other Observational Studies.

Randomized controlled trials

Randomized controlled (field) trials (RCTs), assign persons (conditionally on certain characteristics) randomly to a control group and an intervention group. The randomization ensures that both groups are similar in both observable and unobservable characteristics, given that there are enough participants in the experiment. Differences in outcomes between the intervention and the control group can therefore be attributed solely to the intervention.

Fisher (1925) has shown, more formally, that randomization enables the researcher to quantify the uncertainty associated with the evidence for an effect of a treatment. Specifically, it allows for the calculation of exact p-values of sharp null hypotheses. These p-values are free of assumptions on distributions of outcomes, assumptions on the sampling process, or assumptions on the interaction between persons, solely relying on randomization and a sharp null hypothesis (Imbens, 2009).

Randomized (field) experiments are, however, frequently considered as not possible, uninformative or unethical. Randomization is for example rarely possible with specific macro-economic policies, such as trade, monetary, and fiscal policies (Rodrik, 2008). The results of randomized (field) experiments are, furthermore, often considered to be uninformative when experiments focus on a too specific population, when researchers aim at measuring a local average treatment effect, instead of an average treatment effect, and when experiments are conducted in a too controlled (or laboratory) setting. In these cases, generalization of the research findings might be problematic and the estimated effects may be too narrow to base policy on. It is also commonly remarked that randomized experiments are unethical because one random part of the research population is excluded from participation in a potentially effective intervention.

Quasi experimental studies

Quasi experimental studies (QES) are viewed as credible alternatives for studies that use data from RCTs, for example when RCTs are considered as not possible, uninformative or unethical. In QES, researchers mimic the randomized assignment of the experimental setting, but do so with non-experimental data (Blundell and Costa Dias, 2008). The intervention group includes self-selected persons (for example, students who join a summer school program) or persons who are selected by another process (for example, through a lottery design), along with a control group of persons. Since persons are not randomly distributed over the intervention and the control group, it follows that both groups may have different observable and unobservable characteristics. QES must therefore *demonstrate* that both groups are equivalent on observable characteristics and must *assume* that this equivalence is enough to ensure that both groups are also equivalent on unobservable characteristics. Obviously, the latter cannot be verified, it can only be argued.

Imbens (2009) rightfully remarks that in a situation where one has control over the assignment mechanism, there is little to gain, and much to lose, by giving that up through allowing individuals to choose their own treatment regime. Randomization ensures exogeneity of key variables, where in a corresponding observational study one would have to worry about their endogeneity. Hence, from a first order perspective randomized controlled trials are methodologically superior to observational studies.[5]

But often there is no situation where the researcher has (full) control over the assignment mechanism. In situations where this happens, QES may not only serve as a credible alternative for studies that use data from RCTs, it may even be the best evaluation method at hand.

There are (roughly) five types of QES: (i) natural experiments, (ii) discontinuity design methods, (iii) matching methods, (iv) instrumental variable methods, and (v) difference-in-differences or similar identification methods that rely on panel data. Natural experiments exploit randomization to the intervention created through some naturally occurring event external to the researcher, i.e. forces of nature or a policy change (see, for example, Angrist and Evans, 1998). The line of argumentation of these studies is that persons are randomly allocated to an intervention and a control group due to an exogenous event, such that both groups are equivalent in both observables and unobservables.

Discontinuity design methods exploit 'natural' discontinuities in the rules used to assign individuals to a treatment (see, for example, Lee, 2008). It uses the fact that in highly rule-based worlds, some rules are arbitrary and therefore provide good experiments (Angrist and Pischke, 2009). An example taken from Angrist and Pischke illustrates the discontinuity design method more intuitively. American high school students are awarded National Merit Scholarship Awards on the basis of PSAT scores, a test taken by most college-bound high school juniors, especially those who will later take the SAT. To answer the question if students who win these awards are more likely to finish college one could relate college completion rates to winning the award, but the problem is that students with higher PSAT scores are more likely to finish college. A discontinuity design overcomes this problem by comparing college completion rates of students with PSAT scores around the award cutoff. The discontinuity design therefore compare student groups in the neighborhood of the award cutoff to ensure equivalence in observables and assume equivalence on unobservables.

Matching methods do not use exogenous variation from natural events or natural discontinuities, but instead simulate a control group from the group of non-treated, and re-establishes in this way the experimental conditions in a non-experimental setting. Matching methods rely on observable variables to account for selection issues, and it assumes that the selection on unobservables, that is not accounted for by observables, balances out between the intervention group and the control group (see, for example, Rubin, 1976). Matching methods require rich data, especially on a pretest

---

[5] In the presence of a Hawthorne-effect it may, however, be that RCTs are not superior to QES. The Hawthorne effect is a form of reactivity whereby subjects improve or modify an aspect of their behavior because they are being studied, and not because of the particular incentive they receive during the experiment (see Franke and Kaul, 1978). While in RCTs subjects often are aware of the fact that they are being studied, this is not always the case in QES.

or premeasurement. Otherwise, more complex matching methods are needed in other to evaluate causal mechanisms. De Witte and Van Klaveren (2012), for example, compare dropout rates in two Dutch cities (Amsterdam and Rotterdam) and argue that both student populations are very different in characteristics that may influence the observed dropout rates. To address this problem they perform an iterative matching approach and match a sample of Rotterdam students to the best look-alike sample of students in Amsterdam and repeat this procedure a thousand times. In this way they reconstruct the dropout rate distributions for the student populations in both cities given that the underlying population characteristics are comparable. The matching design therefore enforces equivalence on those observables included in the matching procedure and it is assumed that this is enough to enforce equivalence on unobservables.

Instrumental variable methods (IV) differ from the evaluation methods above, because they focus on the selection on the unobservables. IV requires that there is at least one instrument exclusive to the participation rule. The identifying assumption in IV is that the instrument is only related to the assignment mechanism, and not directly to the outcome variable of interest (see heckman, 1997). Hence, the instrumental variable is assumed to affect the participation rule, which in turn affects the outcome variable. A well known IV study is that of Angrist (1990) who studies the effect of serving in the Vietnam war on the earnings of men. Angrist uses the fact that men were selected based on a lottery draft. This lottery draft was randomly determined and men with a lower draft lottery were more likely to participate in the military. The IV method predicts, in this case, the probability of participation in the military (controlling for observables that affect earnings) and then relates this predicted value to the earnings of men (controlling for observables that affect earnings). Hence, the lottery draft is assumed to affect the participation rule, which in turn affects the earnings of men.

The problem with measuring the effect in the Vietman War study, is that participation in the military is not independent from unobserved factors that affect earnings (even if the researcher controls for observables). In one specific case, the identifying IV assumption is satisfied by construction: randomized (field) trials, where persons are not treated consistent with how they were assigned to the treatment or control group (i.e. there is non-compliance). In this specific situation, the observed participation can be instrumented by how persons were assigned to the treatment. Because the assignment of persons to the treatment was random, it is true by construction that the instrument is only related to the assignment mechanism, and not directly to the outcome variable of interest.

The fifth type of quasi-experimental study is referred to as difference-in-differences (DiD) and rely on panel data. These studies make use of data with a time or cohort dimension to control for unobserved but fixed omitted variables (Angrist and Pischke, 2009). DiD approaches compare persons who are subject to an intervention during a certain time period to other persons who are not subject to the intervention during the same time period. DiD studies must, first of all, show that the intervention and the control group have similar observed characteristics, as well as similar outcomes of interest, before the intervention took place. Secondly, these studies can only argue that the intervention was effective if the measured outcome changes at the moment the intervention group becomes subject to the intervention, while at the same time no such change is observed for the control group.

DiD studies generally use a pre- and post-measurement for both the control and the intervention group, but unlike RCTs, persons are not randomly assigned to both groups. To illustrate the intuition and the shortcomings of DiD we shortly discuss a study of Card and Krueger (1994) who performed a DiD analysis to examine how employment is affected by a dramatic change in the New Jersey state minimum wage, on April 1, 1992. Because fast food restaurants employ many people at the minimum wage, Card and Krueger (1994) collected employment data of fast food restaurants in New Jersey and Pennsylvania, in February 1992 and again in November 1992. The minimum wage in New Jersey increased from $4.25 to $5.05, while the minimum wage in Pennsylvania was $4.25 throughout this period. When they compared the change in employment in New Jersey to the change in employment in Pennsylvania, and controlling for relevant (state) characteristics, they found that the increase in wage increased employment, instead of reduced employment.[6]

The effect found by Card and Krueger (1994) is rather unexpected and it places some doubts on the (internal) validity of the estimated effects. The main problem with DiD analysis is that it is usually very difficult to control for unobserved factors, while (especially for studies more on the macro level) these unobserved factors will likely affect the empirical outcomes. Frequently, DiD studies do not show the trend of the outcome variable, separately for the intervention and the control group, for a long period before and after the change or intervention took place.

Given the frequent lack of longitudinal data, diff-in-diff studies usually do not examine (1) how outcomes fluctuated over time and (2) how these fluctuations influence the estimated effect. In addition the (counterfactual) trend behavior of the intervention and the control group should be the same (Angrist and Pischke, 2009), which is often difficult to argue. DiD analysis is, however, intuitive and the problems mentioned above either also occur with other QES (i.e. equivalence on unobservable cannot be shown) or comes from the fact that longitudinal data is used, which is not a drawback by itself.

A clear distinction should, however, be made between DiD models and other panel data approaches. Panel data studies generally do not define a clear control group and, as a consequence, it is not possible to compare observable characteristics between the intervention and the control group. Moreover, these studies tend to examine how many characteristics influence one single outcome variable. With respect to the internal validity of estimators this is problematic, because the selection mechanism of having a certain characteristic may vary per characteristic. Therefore panel studies that do no adopt a DiD strategy should not be classified as QES and should not be included in a systematic literature review as the empirical results generated by these studies cannot be interpreted causally.

QES differ from RCTs because persons are not randomly assigned to the treatment. Nevertheless, these studies may produce unbiased estimates of the effect of an intervention, and therefore deliver evidence. The quality of the evidence delivered by QES depends on whether the underlying model assumptions are valid, and the main drawback is that equivalence on unobservables between the control and intervention group cannot be shown. It goes beyond the scope of this chapter to discuss each of the quasi experimental evaluation methods in more detail. Thorough surveys of quasi experimental designs are given, among others, by Webbink (2005), Blundell and Costa Dias (2009), Imbens and Wooldridge (2008), Angrist and Pischke (2009) and Imbens (2009).

---

[6] The example is taken from Angrist and Pischke (2009)

Correlational studies

Quantitative correlational studies do not construct a (valid) control group or do not focus on the selection into a certain treatment. This makes these studies fundamentally different from QES and RCTs. Correlational studies examine how observed variation in the measured outcome variable is explained by observed variation of several characteristics and one of these characteristics indicates if a person is treated or not. The focus of these studies is therefore not on the internal validity of estimators and observed outcome differences between the intervention and the (undefined) comparison group may have been caused by the intervention, but also by other (un)observed factors. It follows that correlational studies may produce biased estimates of the effect of the intervention and should not be included in systematic reviews.

It happens far too often that the empirical findings of correlational studies are interpreted as if they represent a causal effect, even though they merely represent a correlation. Moreover, and even worse, many policies are implemented on the basis of correlational studies, while these studies are not informative about the impact of effect of policy measures.

The internal validity of estimators does not play an important role in correlational studies. As a consequence, it is unlikely that correlational studies provide internally valid estimators and that the findings of these studies can be causally interpreted. *The first inclusion criteria is therefore that correlational studies should not be included in systematic literature reviews.*

Based on the discussion of the first order conditions, we conclude that randomized controlled (field) experiments are at the top of the hierarchical ladder when it comes to measuring causal effects. For this reason, randomized control trials are often viewed as the 'golden evaluation standard' (see also the 'Maryland Scale of Scientific Methods, MSSM), but the term golden is misleading as it suggest that findings from randomized controlled trials should always be preferred to the findings from other studies, including those of quasi-experimental studies. In Section 3, where we discuss the second order conditions, we point out that this view is incorrect. QES may provide estimates as reliable as the estimates of the RCT, as long as the underlying model assumptions are valid.

Experimental data are, moreover, often not available and researchers usually do not have control over the assignment mechanism. In these situations QES may not even be a credible alternative for studies that use data from RCTs, it may simply be the best evaluation method at hand. At the same time, and purely from a methodological perspective, it holds that RCTs are superior to QES, because QES must *demonstrate* that the intervention and control group are equivalent on observable characteristics and must *assume* that this equivalence ensures equivalence on unobservable characteristics. The latter assumption cannot be formally tested. Also RCTs should demonstrate equivalence of observables between the control group and the intervention group to show that the randomization was successful. *The second inclusion criteria therefore is that RCTs and QES must show the equivalence on observables between control and intervention group.* This condition includes that the IV studies should make plausible that the instrument is only related to the assignment mechanism, and not directly to the outcome variable of interest.

Differences in the methodological approach adopted may lead to differences in the estimated effect. It is, for example, difficult to check if a study uses a valid instrument, and the decision on whether a study uses a valid instrument is at least subjective. It is therefore important that systematic reviews verify if the estimated effects depend on the chosen methodological approach. Systematic reviews should therefore present information on the used methodological approach of the reviewed study.

3. Second order conditions

Second order conditions are conditions related to analytical and data issues of the reviewed studies. Data issues or analytical deficiencies may be independent of the research methodology used, but can bias the estimated effectiveness of an intervention.

In Table 1-1 we present a list of second order problems that may occur, like, attrition, missing values, (non-)clustered standard errors, learning effects, equivalence of the intervention and control group, problems with the validity of the used instrument to identify the effect of the intervention and problems with the power of the analysis (i.e. small sample bias). Some of these second order deficiencies are relatively easy to address. For example, in randomized experiments it may be difficult to reject the null hypothesis that the intervention is not effective due to a small sample size. By reporting the power of the test, authors can show that the estimated effect is large enough to reject the null hypothesis, even though the sample size is small.

Unfortunately, not all second order deficiencies can be easily addressed. For example, the validity of an instrument cannot be formally shown, it can only be argued by the authors. Sometimes it is obvious that an instrument is valid (e.g. participation status is instrumented by the random assignment status when there is litle non-compliance), but it may not be so obvious in other cases (e.g. the Vietnam lottery example of Section 2). Subjective discussions on the validity of instruments are informative, but are not usefull for defining inclusion criteria that determine when studies are to be included in a literature review.

Data Problems	Analytical Problems
Small sample size	Standard errors (not) clustered
Attrition	Same Pre- and Post-test (learning effects)
Missing values/information	Equivalence of intervention and control group not shown
No common support	Nonvalid Instrument
Contamination	Power of the test not calculated
Cross-over effects	

Table 1-1 List of (some) second order problems

The difficulty with second order deficiencies is that it is generally not clear how they bias the estimated effectiveness of an intervention. It is possible that a well designed QES provides a more accurate estimate than a methodologically superior RCT, due to more (unobserved) second order problems in the RCT-study. The difference between the estimated and true effectiveness can only be determined if the true effect of the intervention is known, and only then it would be possible to examine which studies provided the most accurate estimates. It follows that second order deficiencies, and their unknown consequences, for the estimates make it impossible to rank studies purely based on the chosen evaluation method. To judge the quality of evidence that is delivered by the included studies, it is necessary to evaluate and report data and analytical problems in systematic literature reviews.

To minimize the effect of second order problems we propose a third and a fourth inclusion criteria. *The third inclusion criteria is that studies must be accepted for publication in international and peer-reviewed journals or must be published as a chapter in a peer-reviewed thesis.* The intuition underlying this inclusion criteria is that reviewers, editors, promoters and committee members recognize analytical and data problems such that these problems are better addressed.

This criteria is, however, controversial due to the well-known publication bias that may bias the estimated effectiveness of an intervention. It has been shown that studies are more likely to be published if the empirical findings suggest that an outcome variable is positively and significantly influenced by the intervention studied (Slavin, 2008). Considering only published and peer-reviewed studies in systematic literature reviews would then impose an upward bias on the estimated effectiveness of the intervention studied. The third inclusion criteria therefore implies that the problem of having analytical and data deficiencies is substituted for the problem of having publication bias. A major advantage of this inclusion criteria, however, is that the possible impact of publication bias is verifiable, while the possible impact of second order deficiencies are not verifiable. To have an idea of the impact of publication bias it is important that systematic literature reviews verify how findings of non-published studies that satisfy the first two inclusion criteria compare to the findings of the studies that are included in the systematic literature review. Differences between the findings of these unpublished studies and the studies included in the systematic literature review are then either caused by publication bias or by second order deficiencies. The larger this difference is, the more skeptical one should be about the reliability of the estimated effectiveness of the intervention.

It is noteworthy that small sample experiments in medicine frequently find huge effect sizes and it is often reasoned that publication bias is a more serious problem in small sample research than in studies with large samples (Givens and Tweedie, 1997, Sterne, Gavaghan and Egger, 2000, Rothstein, Sutton and Borenstein, 2005). Therefore, the sample size of each study should be reported in a systematic literature review.

The fourth inclusion criteria is that the focus of the literature review must be congruent to the focus of the studies included in the review. Studies often control for several characteristics that may affect the outcome variable, besides the intervention. The first and second order problems are usually not addressed for these control variables, but are only addressed for the evaluated intervention. Studies that are interested in the effectiveness of the intervention, frequently also show and discuss how different control variables affect the outcome variable. The estimates of these control variables can obviously not be interpreted as evidence.

4. Third order conditions

Third order conditions are related to the representativeness or usefullness of the empirical findings of studies that are included in systematic literature reviews (i.e. the findings of studies that satisfy the first four inclusion criteria). These conditions enfold the issues of external validity, effect size and informativeness for the actual implementation of a program. We subsequently discuss each of these three issues, starting with *external validity*.

RCTs and QES value the internal validity of estimates more than the external validity of estimates, and reliable estimates for specific subpopulations are therefore preferred to representative but unreliable estimates for the overall population. It is, however, unclear how representative findings for one subpopulation are for another (sub)population. To give an extreme example, if the findings of a perfectly conducted randomized controlled trial in KwaZulu-Natal (province of South Africa) indicate that a summer school program was effective, then this (obviously) does not mean that a similar summer school program will be effective in New York as well. The value of empirical evidence thus depends on what the evidence is needed for and how it will be used (see also Rodrik, 2008, who has a similar argument).

Even though there is a debate on whether internal validity should be preferred over external validity (see Banerjee and Duflo, 2008), this discussion is not so relevant for the inclusion of studies in systematic literature reviews. Internally valid estimators are estimators that are reliable given the specific conditions under which the study was performed. It applied that the representativeness of estimates for other populations is in the `eye of the beholder'. A summer school evaluation for Amsterdam is likely to be more representative for New York than a summer school evaluation for KwaZulu-Natal, but policy makers and researchers in New York can probably judge best on how representative the empirical findings are. It therefore implies that systematic reviews should present information on the research population used in the included studies, but no inclusion criteria can be formulated on the basis of external validity.

The second issue concerns the relevance of effect sizes in systematic literature reviews. Literature reviews (and meta-analysis) often conveniently use standardized effect sizes to label the empirical evidence as weak, moderate or strong.[7] These effect sizes quantify the impact that an intervention has on the outcome variable, and enables comparison across studies and across interventions. The latter gives information on which intervention is the more effective one.

Reviews usually tend to focus on `what works' and associate larger effect sizes with stronger evidence. A consequence is that studies with negative or zero effect sizes are less often mentioned in review reports. The 'what works'-paradigm implies a risk for falsification (ignoring Popper's 'black swan') and may give a misleading message about the effectiveness of a certain intervention to policy makers and educational practitioners. Information on the ineffectiveness of interventions is equally informative than information on the effectiveness of interventions and systematic reviews should therefore include studies irrespective of the effect size they find.

---

[7] See, for example, the 'Best Evidence Encyclopedia' (www.bestevidence.org).

Two practical problems with effect sizes are that (a) studies frequently do not report them (nor the statistics needed to calculate one) and (b) that there is no consensus about what an effect size represents and how it should be calculated. To illustrate the latter: effects sizes are defined using Cohen's d (Cohen and Cohen, 1983), or Hedges' g (Hedges, 1981), or are defined as *the proportion of a standard deviation by which the experimental group outperformed the control group (adjusting for any pretest differences)* (www.bestevidence.org). An advantage of reporting effect sizes is that empirical findings of different empirical studies can be compared, but this advantage disappears when different effect-size definitions are used. Systematic reviews should thus report effect sizes and the definition of these effect sizes.

A third issue relates to the similarity between the evaluated programs and the programs that people plan to implement (on a large scale). Review studies should therefore provide information about cost effectiveness and upscaling possibilities. The importance of this issue can be illustrated by the following example. Suppose that a summer school program was evaluated by a well designed RCT. To guarantee that the experiment was properly conducted each student in the summer school program was guided by a university student. The experimental results show that the summer school is effective, however the effectiveness may be caused by the intensive personal guidance rather than by the summer school program. If the summer school program would be implemented on a large scale, such intensive guidance would be practically undoable and too costly. Hence the experiment practically has no value because the evaluated program will never be implemented in practice.

Again, judgements on cost-effectiveness, implementation and upscaling is in the eye of the beholder (i.e. different persons may have different opinions on what, for example, cost-effectiveness is). Systematic reviews should therefore be as informative as possible on these issues, but the inclusion criteria of systematic reviews should be independent from these issues because the internal validity of the estimated effectiveness is independent from these issues.

5. Applying the inclusion criteria in practice

This section examines to what extent systematic literature reviews already apply the four defined inclusion criteria, and if systematic reviews provide information about external validity, effect sizes and cost-effectiveness. For this purpose we examine the applied inclusion criteria and the information provided by a series of articles in Review of Educational Research. This journal specialized in systematic literature reviews and publishes articles that come from various social science disciplines, namely pedagogy, sociology, psychology and economics. In particular we examined all review studies that were published in 2010 in this journal.

By comparing the derived inclusion criteria in this study with the inclusion criteria used by the reviews published in Review of Educational Research we obtain more insight on (1) whether there is consensus about the inclusion criteria that should be used, and on (2) the completeness and consistency of the applied inclusion criteria in systematic reviews.

Under the assumption that the derived inclusion criteria in this study are correct, it furthermore gives an impression of the extent to which systematic reviews focus on 'evidence' (i.e. internal validity) and if these reviews provide information that is relevant for the implementation of (policy) interventions.

Reviews in Review of Educational Research

18 review studies were published in Review of Education Research in 2010. The inclusion criteria used in these studies varied from 1 to 7, and studies used 3.7 inclusion criteria on average. Appendix A provides a detailed description of the applied inclusion criteria by these 18 reviews.

1-2 shows if the published review studies applied the inclusion criteria derived in this study. The columns indicate each inclusion criteria that systematic litearture reviews should adopt:

I. Include only RCTs and QES.
II. Include only RCTs and QES that show the equivalence on observables between of the control and the intervention group.
III. Include only published and peer-reviewed studies (or theses)
IV. Include only studies that focus specifically on the topic reviewed.

The table indicates Y(es) if a study satisfies the inclusion criteria, and N(o) otherwise. The bottom row of Table 1-2 indicates the percentage of studies that satisfied the first, second, third and fourth inclusion criteria, respectively.

The table clearly shows that none of the reviews apply all four inclusion criteria, which indicates that it is not common practice to apply the four derived inclusion criteria. Two thirds of the reviews included only studies that specifically focus on the review topic (i.e. inclusion criteria IV.). These reviews generally do not provide an argument for applying this inclusion criteria; it is just applied withouth any argument, or it is viewed as a logic consequence of the search strategy that authors used in their review. Those review studies that gave an argument for not applying the fourth inclusion criteria mentioned that this broadened the number of studies in the review. Thereby, these studies attach more value to increasing the number of studies than to including studies that better address data and analytical problems.

Five of the 18 review studies (28 percent) include only peer reviewed articles. These reviews all argue that quality of peer reviewed articles is guaranteed, while there are no quarantees in the 'gray' literature. The main arguments of review studies to include also non-published studies are (a) to avoid possible selection bias and (b) because this inclusion criterion reduces the number of studies that can be selected. Section 3 explains that analytical and data deficiencies are reduced by including only published and peer-reviewed studies, but that this choice, at the same time, increases the likelihood of having publication bias. Review studies should therefore compare the findings of unpublished studies and published studies (given that these studies satisfy the other formulated inclusion criteria). Differences in research findings are then either caused by publication bias or by second order deficiencies, and the larger this difference the more sceptical one should be about the reliability of the estimated effectiveness of the intervention. One could, for example, define a reliability index that divides the estimated impact of published studies by the estimated impact by non-published studies. This reliability index would then indicate 1 if the estimated impact by published studies is similar to that of non-published studies.

Finally, the table shows that only 3 review studies (17 percent) exclude correlational studies. Review studies that exclude correlational studies also include only (quasi) experimental designs with well matched treatment and control groups. It seems to be the case that if studies satisfy inclusion criteria II, they automatically satisfy inclusion criteria I. Review studies that do not satisfy the first two inclusion criteria do not provide evidence because the reviewed studies do not focus on the internal validity of estimators.

		Inclusion criteria			
Authors	**Pages**	I.	II.	III.	IV.
Bowman	4-33	N	N	N	N
Cooper et al.	34-70	N	N	N	Y
Achinstein et al.	71-107	N	N	N	Y
Superfine	108-137	N	N	Y	Y
Bowers et al.	144-197	N	N	Y	Y
Ngan Ng et al.	180-206	N	N	Y	Y
Adesope et al.	207-245	Y	Y	N	N
Mills	246-271	N	N	Y	N
Crede et al.	272-295	N	N	N	N
Marulis et al.	300-335	Y	Y	N	Y
Cavagnetto	336-371	N	N	Y	Y
Rakes et al.	372-400	Y	Y	N	Y
Patall et al.	401-437	N	N	N	Y
Goldrick-Rap	437-469	N	N	N	Y
Holme	476-526	N	N	N	Y
Johnson	527-575	N	N	N	N
Bohnert et al.	576-610	N	N	N	Y
Lovett	611-638	N	N	N	N
Total		17%	17%	28%	67%

Table 1-2 Applied inclusion criteria by studies published in Review of Education Research 2010

Table 1-2 suggests that 3 of the 18 review studies potentially provide evidence because they satisfy the first two inclusion criteria. None of these studies include only published studies which reduces possible publication bias, but which, at the same time, increases the likelihood that data and analytical problems are not properly addressed. Two of the three more causally oriented literature reviews include studies that do not specifically focus on the topic reviewed. This may bias the review findings because data and analytical problems may not be properly addressed (see section 3).

Table 1-3 shows whether the 18 review studies provide information on external validity, effect sizes and cost-effectiveness or up-scaling possibilities. Section 4 argues that this information is essential for making an informative choice between different potentially effective interventions and the implementation of these specific interventions.

The table shows that it is not common practice for review studies to provide this information. Less than 50 percent of the review studies report effect sizes. Some reviews mention that they only report effect sizes if possible, which points to the fact that effect sizes are not always given or cannot always be calculated from the study reviewed. The absence of effect sizes makes it more difficult to compare differences in the measured intervention impact of the reviewed studies.

Only 7 of the 19 review articles (39%) described the research populations of the reviewed studies. As a consequence, the value of the delivered empirical evidence by these review studies remains unclear, because, in the end, this value depends on what the evidence is needed for and how it will be used.

Finally, Table 1-3 shows that information on the cost-effectiveness and up-scaling possibilities is never presented in the reviews (last column). One of the probable reasons is that the reviewed studies do not provide this information, as is suggested by Marulis et al. (2010).

Authors	pages	external validity	effect sizes	cost-effectiveness/ implementation
Bowman	4-33	N	Y	N
Cooper et al.	34-70	N	Y	N
Achinstein et al.	71-107	N	N	N
Superfine	108-137	N	N	Y
Bowers et al.	144-197	Y	Y	N
Ngan Ng et al.	180-206	N	N	N
Adesope et al.	207-245	Y	Y	N
Mills	246-271	N	N	N
Crede et al.	272-295	N	N	N
Marulis et al.	300-335	Y	Y	N
Cavagnetto	336-371	N	N	N
Rakes et al.	372-400	Y	Y	N
Patall et al.	401-437	N	N	N
Goldrick-Rap	437-469	Y	N	N
Holme	476-526	N	Y	N
Johnson	527-575	N	N	N
Bohnert et al.	576-610	Y	Y	N
Lovett	611-638	Y	N	N
Total		39%	44%	6%

Table 1-3 Information provided in literature reviews in Review of Education Research 2010

6. Concluding remarks

Systematic reviews that focus on internal validity generally include studies based on rather ad hoc inclusion criteria which may lead to inconsistencies in the outcomes generated by these reviews. Currently there is no predefined set of inclusion criteria and there two reasons for this. First of all, many evaluation approaches on causal inference were developed in the last two decades and, second of all, there are often few experimental studies. The formulation of consistent and transparent inclusion criteria is therefore difficult.

The objective of this study is to derive a set of inclusion criteria from the theoretical literature on causal inference. Thereby this study contributes to the literature by providing more consistent and transparant inclusion criteria which should increase the extent to which systematic reviews provide evidence. The second contribution of this study is that it presents study characteristics that reviews should minimally provide to the reader (if possible) in order to be informative that also follow from the methodological discussion on causal inference. The presented inclusion criteria and study characteristics are, furthermore, of practical value for policy makers, principals and teachers, as it provides them with an easy-to-apply list of rules that can be used to review empirical studies for evidence based policy or evidence based practise.

This study derives the following set of inclusion criteria from the theoretical literature on causal inference:

I. Include experimental or quasi-experimental studies only.
II. Include experimental or quasi-experimental studies that show the equivalence on observables of the control and the intervention group.
III. Include only published and peer-reviewed studies (or theses).
IV. Include only studies that focus specifically on the topic reviewed.

The characteristics that systematic reviews should minimally provide (if available) in order to be informative are:
- *[Identification]:* The adopted identification method
- *[external validity:]* The research population, conditions and publication year;
- *[effect size:]* The (standardized) effect size(s) and type of effect size;
- *[Implementability:]* Information on cost-effectiveness and upscaling possibilities.
- *[publication bias:]* A comparisson of the findings of published and non-published studies that satisfy inclusion criteria I, II and IV.

These characteristics are not related to the internal valididy of the estimated effect and are, therefore, not considered as inclusion criteria. However, showing these characteristics is extremely important for a better understanding of causal mechanisms and for using the review results for evidence based policy.

Finally this study examined to what extent systematic literature reviews already apply the four defined inclusion criteria and show the study characteristics indicated by this study. For this purpose we reviewed all 18 published review studies in Review of Education Research in 2010.

The inclusion criteria seem minimal and straightforward, yet only three of the 18 review studies satisfy the first two inclusion criteria. None of these three review studies included only published studies and 33 percent of the review studies included studies that do not focus specifically on the topic reviewed. The comparisson indicates that it is not common practice to apply the four inclusion criteria derived in this study. Consequently, the results generated by these studies provide no causal evidence, but provide correlations which cannot be used by policy makers for evidence based policy.

With respect to the reported study characteristics we conclude that less than 50% of the review studies report information on effect sizes or external validity and only 1 study reported information concerning the implementability. The latter result is likely because the studies selected in review studies usually do not report information on implementability. As a consequence, the policy value of the generated result often remains unclear, because, in the end, this value depends on what the evidence is needed for and how it will be used.

Finally, we would like to discuss two issues with respect to the derived inclusion criteria in this study. First of all, the choice to include only published and peer-reviewed studies in systematic reviews is controversial. It may impose a publication bias and at the same time it reduces the probability that the empirical results are driven by analytical and data deficiencies. Therefore, we added the study characteristic that results of published and unpublished studies that satisfy inclusion criteria I, II and IV should be compared. One should be more sceptical about the reliability of the review findings as the difference between the outcomes of published and unpublished studies becomes larger.

A second issue is that there are frequently no or few experimental or quasi-experimental studies available. Applying the inclusion criteria derived in this study would mean that systematic literature reviews can select no or only a few. At this point it is relevant to recognize the main objective of this study: deriving a set of consistent and transparant inclusion criteria from the theoretical literature on *causal inference*. If the best evidence is delivered by non-causal studies, then our study does not indicate that reviewing these studies is uninformative. Instead it suggests that systematic reviews that evaluate the outcomes of these studies are uninformative with respect to the underlying causal mechanism. In our opinion, these literature reviews should mention explicitly that the review outcomes may not be suitable for evidence-based policy making.

References

Angrist, J. and W. Evans (1998). Children and their parents' labor supply: Evidence from exogenous variation in family size. *American Economic Review, 88*(3), 450-477.

Angrist, J.D. and A.B. Krueger (1999). Empirical Strategies in Labor Economics, volume 3 of Handbook of Labor Economics, chapter 23, pages 1277-1364. Elsevier Science B.V.

Angrist, J.D. and J.S. Pischke. Mostly harmless econometrics: an empiricist's companion. Princeton, NJ [u.a.]: Princeton Univ. Press, 2009. ISBN 978-0-691-12035-5.

Banerjee, A. and E. Duflo (2008). The experimental approach to development economics. NBER Working Papers 14467, National Bureau of Economic Research, Inc.

Blundell, R. and M. Costa Dias (2009). Alternative approaches to evaluation in empirical microeconomics. *Journal of Human Resources, 44*(3), 565-640.

Card, D., and A. Krueger (1994). Minimum Wages and Employment: A Case Study of the Fast Food Industry in New Jersey and Pennsylvania, American Economic Review, 84, 772-784.

Cohen, J. and P. Cohen. Applied multiple regression/correlation analysis for the behavioral sciences. Technical report, (2nd ed.) Hillsdale, NJ: Erlbaum, 1983.

De Witte, K. and C. Van Klaveren (2012) Comparing students by a matching analysis: on early school leaving in Dutch cities. *Applied Economics, 44*(28), 3679-3690.

Fisher, R.A. The design of experiment. 1st ed., Oliver and Boyd, London, 1925.

Franke, R.H. and J.D. Kaul (1978). The Hawthorne experiments: First statistical interpretation. *American Sociological Review, 43*(5), 623-643.

Givens, G.H., D.D. Smith, and R.L. Tweedie (1997). Publication bias in meta-analysis: a Bayesian data-augmentation approach to account for issues exemplified in the passive smoking debate (with discussion). *Statistical Science, 12*, 221-250.

Greene, J. P., and M.A. Winters (2007). Revisiting grade retention: An evaluation of Florida's test based promotion policy. *Education Finance and Policy, 2*(4), 319-340.

Heckman, J. (1997). Instrumental variables: A study of implicit behavioral assumptions used in making program evaluations. *Journal of Human Resources, 2*(3), 441-462.

Hedges, L.V. (1981).Distribution theory for glass's estimator of effect size and related estimators. *Journal of Educational Statistics, 6*(2), 107-128.

Holland, P.W. (1986) Statistics and causal inference (with discussion). Journal of the *American Statistical Association, 81*, 945-970.

Imbens, G.W. (2009). Better late than nothing: some comments on Deaton (2009) and Heckman and Urzua 2009. NBER Working Papers 14896, National Bureau of Economic Research, Inc.

Imbens, G.W. and J.M. Wooldridge (2008) Recent developments in the econometrics of program evaluation. IZA Discussion Papers 3640.

Lee, D.S. (2008). Randomized experiments from non-random selection in U.S. house elections. *Journal of Econometrics, 142*(2), 675-697.

Ou, S. R., and A.J. Reynolds (2010). Grade retention, postsecondary education, and public aid receipt. *Educational Evaluation and Policy Analysis, 32*(1), 118-139.

Rodrik, D. (2008).The new development economics: We shall experiment, but how shall we learn? Working Paper Series rwp08-055, Harvard University, John F.Kennedy School of Government.

Rothstein, H.R., A.J. Sutton, and M. Borenstein. Publication bias in meta-analysis: Prevention, assessment, and adjustments. Chichester, UK: John Wiley., 2005.

Roy, A. (1951). Some thoughts on the distribution of earnings. *Oxford Economic Papers, 3*, 135-146.

Rubin, D.B. (1974). Estimating causal effects and treatments in randomized and non randomized studies. *Journal of Educational Psychology, 66*, 688-701.

Rubin, D.B. (1976). Inference and missing data. *Biometrika, 63*, 581-592.

Slavin, R.E. (1984). Meta-analysis in education: How has it been used? *Educational Researcher, 13*, 6-15.

Slavin, R.E. (1986). Best evidence synthesis: An alternative to meta-analysis and traditional reviews. *Educational Researcher, 15*, 5-11.

Slavin, R.E. (2008) What works? Issues in synthesizing educational program evaluations. *Educational Researcher, 37*, 5-14.

Neyman, J. (1990). On the principles of probability theory to agricultural experiments. essays on principles. section 9. *Statistical Sciences, 5*, 465-471.

Sterne, J., D. Gavaghan, and M. Egger (2000). Publication and related bias in meta-analysis: power of statistical tests and prevalence in literature. *Journal of Clinical Epidemiology, 53*, 1119-1129.

Van Klaveren, C. and K. De Witte (2012). Football to improve math and reading performance. Tier Working Paper 12-07, 1-22.

Webbink, D. (2005). Causal effects in education. *Journal of Economic Surveys, 19*(4), 535-560.

What Works Clearinghouse. Procedures and standards handbook. Technical report, Retrieved December, 2008.

Wooldridge, J.M. (2001). Econometric Analysis of Cross Section and Panel Data. MIT Press Books, The MIT Press, edition 1, volume 1, number 0262232197.

Appendix A. Inclusion criteria used in review articles in the Review of Education, edition 2010

paper by	pages	Inclusion criteria
Bowman	4-33	- participants were undergraduate students or were reporting about their previous undergraduate experiences in the United States, - at least one independent variable measured a college diversity experience, - the DV measured cognitive skills or tendencies, and - statistics regarding the magnitude of the effect were provided.
Cooper et al.	34-70	- the study had to have focused on the difference between kindergarten programs that operated on a half-day schedule versus a full-day schedule on a measure of student academic achievement or readiness, some other measure of student development or well-being, or some measure of classroom process. - no studies that compared HDK to FDK that met on alternating school days. - studies had to study kindergarten programs based in the United States or Canada. - no studies that intentionally confounded the FDK variable with another instructional intervention. - outcomes measured at the end of the kindergarten year or the beginning of first grade. - enough information to permit the calculation of an estimate of the relationship between the length of the kindergarten day and the outcome measure.
Achinstein et al.	71-107	- reported an empirical study, - adhered to the American Educational Research Association's (2006) published standards for reporting on empirical social science research, and - informed an important aspect of retention of new teachers of color, such as retention rates and turnover factors.
Superfine	108-137	- directly applied to the focus of this review - authoritative nature of the literature (i.e., publication in a peer-reviewed journal, publication at a major academic press, or including extensive references to such sources in the case of law review articles), and - its relevance to issues of centralization and decentralization of authority.

Bowers et al.	144	- Published in English, reporting on research carried out in an alphabetic orthography - Investigated instruction with elementary school students, - Investigated instruction about any element of oral or written morphology, - At least one third of the instruction was focused on morphology, based on the intervention description, - Reported literacy outcome measures with means and standard deviations for comparison, - Used either an experimental and control or comparison group or a training group with pre- and posttests using measures that could be compared to established norms
Ngan Ng et al.	180-206	- no conference papers, book reviews and unpublished materials. - no chapters that reported on sets of data in published studies that we had previously reviewed.
Adesope et al.	207-245	- Bilingual participants were reported to be equally (or almost equally) proficient in two languages. Bilinguals with learning disabilities or other cognitive disabilities were excluded. - They had an experimental group of bilingual participants and a control group of monolingual participants. - Measured outcomes (cognitive benefits) were clearly reported. - They reported sufficient data to allow for effect size calculations. - They were publicly available, either online or in library archives.
Mills	246-271	- timeframe of 1999 through 2009 - observational studies
Crede et al.	272-295	- report correlations between either (a) class attendance and college GPA or (b) attendance in a particular class and the grade obtained in that class or allowed computation of either of these relationships. - no laboratory studies or attendance in high school or primary school classes. - not if only statistically significant findings were reported - no articles where the grade in a class was based, in part, on class attendance.

Marulis et al.	300-335	- the study included a training, intervention, or specific teaching technique to increase word learning; - a (quasi)experimental design was applied, incorporating one or more of the following: a randomized controlled trial, a pretest–intervention–posttest with a control group, or a postintervention comparison between preexisting groups; - participants had no mental, physical, or sensory handicaps and were within ages birth through 9; - the study was conducted with English words, excluding foreign language or nonsense words (to be able to make comparable comparisons across studies); and - outcome variables included a dependent variable that measured word learning, identified as either expressive or receptive vocabulary development or both.
Cavagnetto	336-371	- only articles that established a connection between argument and scientific literacy or the nature of science were used. -articles reporting on research associated with argument-based interventions or a component of the intervention (articles from peer-reviewed practitioner journals were not included), - articles that offered a clear description of the intervention, and - articles reporting on interventions designed for K–12 students.
Rakes et al.	372-400	- the intervention had to target the learning of algebraic concepts, regardless of the title of the classes being examined. - the intervention had to involve a method for improving learning as measured by student achievement - employ an (quasi)experimental design with a comparison group. - the comparison group had to have received the "usual" instruction.
Patall et al.	401-437	- focus on the differences between students attending ED or EY schools and students at traditional day or year schools, - a naturally occurring measure of number of school days or hours in the school day and its relationship to student achievement, or - a description of programs that implemented changes in the length of the year or length of the day. - appeared in 1985 or after. - programs based in the United States or Canada. - no studies examining the effect of full-day versus half-day kindergarten

Goldrick-Rab	437-469	- they used quantitative or qualitative methods that could rigorously address the research questions, and - quantitative studies needed to produce findings that could reasonably be generalized beyond the sample to the larger population of community college students. - sufficient and appropriate data, following a research design that made it possible to answer the questions posed and a transparent and defensible approach to sampling and data collection.
Holme	476-526	- *relevance*: only studies that pertained to the issue of exit testing for a high school diploma and that were relevant to our four central questions. We excluded studies that focused on students with disabilities and studies that focused on measurement and validity issues related to exit exams. - *empirical nature*: both qualitative and quantitative studies that reported original research rather than the research of others, prior research, or opinion. - *scholarship quality*, studies must have (a) provided a clear and well-supported logic of inquiry, (b) adequately described the design and sources of evidence, (c) used sources of evidence that were appropriate to the scope of the questions, (d) described the analysis procedures, and (e) described the warrants for conclusions.
Johnson	527-575	- neighborhood features or residency as predictors or treatments; - outcomes that were measures of achievement, psychosocial dispositions toward education, matriculation, or learning behaviors; - contemporary U.S. populations sampled circa 1960 or later; and - estimates of neighborhood influences for African Americans.
Bohnert et al.	576-610	- utilized at least one of the dimensions of involvement (i.e., breadth, intensity, duration, engagement). - both quantitative and qualitative in nature and utilized survey, experience sampling, time-use diaries, and observational methods for data collection.
Lovett	611-638	- none

CHAPTER 2

Selection Bias in Educational Issues and the Use of Heckman's Sample Selection Model

Nick Deschacht[1], Katie Goeman [2] [3]

1. Introduction

This chapter discusses the importance of sample selection bias in educational research issues and the use of Heckman's sample selection model in the literature on education economics. We carried out a systematic literature review on the use of Heckman's model in the field of educational research to investigate which research topics are studied, how the problem of sample selection bias is addressed, how the results of Heckman models are presented and interpreted and how these models re-adjust previous findings. The next paragraph introduces the problem of causal inference and the nature of sample selection bias. Paragraph 3 provides a non-mathematical introduction to the sample selection model. Paragraph 4 presents the literature review and the last paragraph sums up the main findings and conclusions.

2. Selection bias and causality

Introductory examples

The classic example of sample selection bias deals with the effect of education on wages or earnings. It is this example that led James Heckman to develop his sample selection model during the 1970s. There is a long standing debate among economists on whether educational levels causally determine earnings, as human capital theorists claim. Sceptics would argue that education in itself does not lead to higher earnings, but merely acts as a signal of higher productivity which employers use in hiring decisions. The debate raises a simple empirical question: how big or small is the effect of additional education on earnings? A (too) simple strategy to measure this effect would be to compare the mean earnings of a group of high educated employees (say $\bar{y}_{high}$) to the mean earnings of a group of low-educated employees ($\bar{y}_{low}$). If we call $\hat{\beta}_{OLS}$ the estimated effect of education

---

[1] Corresponding author: nick.deschacht@kuleuven.be. KU Leuven, Faculty of Economics and Business, Warmoesberg 26, 1000 Brussels, Belgium.
[2] KU Leuven, Faculty of Economics and Business, Educational Research and Development, Warmoesberg 26, 1000 Brussels, Belgium.
[3] Faculty of Psychology and Pedagogical Sciences, Centre for Instructional Psychology and Technology, Dekenstraat 2, 3000 Leuven, Belgium.

on earnings using this strategy, this estimate can be written as $\hat{\beta}_{OLS} = \bar{y}_{high} - \bar{y}_{low}$. The exact same estimate of the effect can be obtained by a regression analysis in which the earnings of each employee in the sample (y_i) are regressed on a dummy variable D_i taking the value 0 if the employee is low-educated and 1 if the employee is high educated. If the model $y_i = \beta_0 + \beta_{OLS} D_i + \epsilon_i$ is estimated using OLS, then the estimated coefficient of the educational dummy will equal $\hat{\beta}_{OLS}$, which is why we introduced the index 'OLS' to denote this estimator. The regression framework is equivalent to estimating the effect as the simple difference in mean earnings of the high- and low-educated in the sample, but regression has the advantage that it can easily be extended to a multivariate setting in which other relevant characteristics (such as experience or the sector of employment) can be held constant in the analysis.

There are well-known shortcomings to this estimation strategy such as the role of omitted variables. But during the 1970s scholars began to realize that yet another mechanism could be leading to systematically wrong estimates (i.e. $\hat{\beta}_{OLS}$ could be biased): 'sample selectivity'. This potential bias results from the fact that calculating $\hat{\beta}_{OLS}$ requires data on the earnings of people, because earnings data are by definition missing for people who are not working and workers are not representative for the whole population. (At this point it is important to note that missing data are a necessary condition for sample selection bias but not a sufficient condition, we return to this issue later.) The issue of missing earnings data was especially relevant in the case of women, whose participation rates in the labour force were well below those of men in the 1970s.

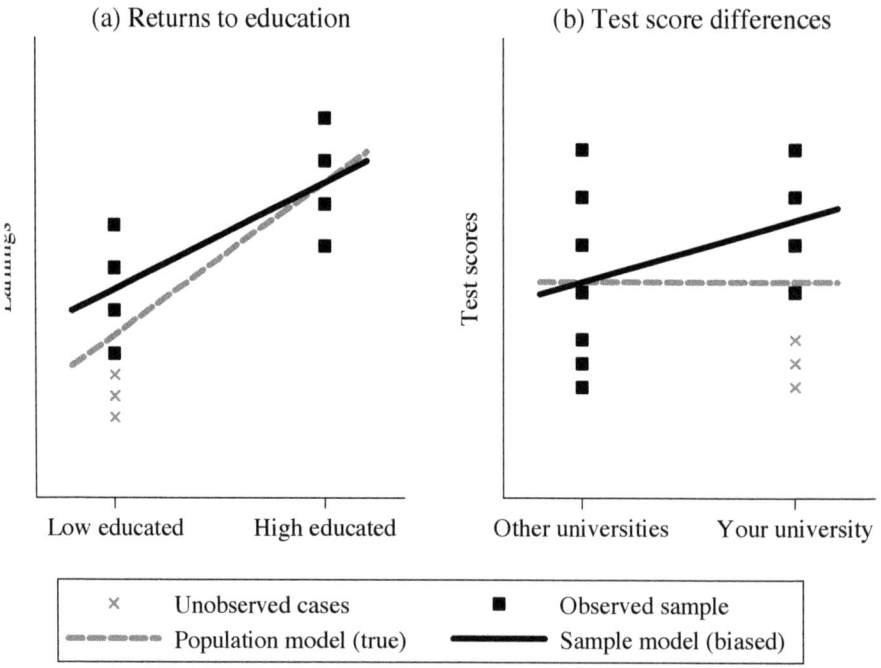

Figure 2-1 Two examples of sample selection bias

Figure 1(a) illustrates how sample selection bias may arise when measuring the effect of education on earnings. The observations in the sample are shown as black squares: these represent female workers for whom we observe earnings. The grey crosses represent women who are not working and whose wages are therefore not observed in the sample. The grey crosses show the potential wages of the unobserved cases, i.e. the wage these non-working women would earn if they would work. The dashed line is a fit line of which the slope shows the true effect of education on female earnings in the total population, while the black line is the fit line based on the observed sample only. The slopes of the fit lines represent the estimated effects of education on earnings. As drawn, the dashed line is steeper than the black line which implies that the true effect of education on earnings is greater than a researcher would suspect based on a sample of workers only (so the estimate is biased). The unobserved cases are not randomly scattered over the plot: the non-workers are predominantly low-educated people with low potential earnings compared to the other low-educated. It is important to understand that sample selection bias in this case is not caused by the mere fact that the higher educated are more likely to work, but by the fact that those low-educated women who do work are likely to score well on some unmeasured characteristic. Consider the role of another variable 'ability' – the general level of competence or intelligence – which is a variable we do not observe. Assume that ability tends to increase earnings and that ability increases the probability to work and so to be selected in the sample. The low-educated women who score high on ability are more likely to work and earn relatively high wages. The low-educated women who score low on ability and therefore have low potential wages, are less likely to work. The underestimation of the effect of education on earnings in the sample, the sample selection bias, thus results from the fact that low-educated women are less likely to work and that those low-educated women who do work have relatively high levels of ability and earnings.

The sample selection bias in the example in Figure 1(a) cannot be removed by weighting the sample. Weighting is a common – and often useful – procedure when a sample is not representative for the population one is studying. In Figure 1(a) it is clear that the low-educated are underrepresented in the sample. By giving the observed low-educated respondents in the sample a greater weight, the sample can be re-balanced so that the proportion of low-educated in the sample would equal the proportion of low-educated in the population. However, weighting the sample would replace the unobserved grey crosses in Figure 1(a) by the observed black squares, i.e. by respondents with higher potential earnings than the unobserved cases. The estimated effect of education on earnings after weighting would still be the (biased) black fit line. Thus, weighting is no solution for the problem of sample selection bias.

We now consider another example in which an educational variable takes the role of the dependent variable rather than the explanatory variable. There is large literature in educational economics on the determinants of student test scores. Suppose you want to compare the exam scores of students for one of your courses with the scores of students for a similar exam at other universities. The mean score of the students at your university is greater than the mean score at other universities, which at first sight appears to show that you are a great teacher. However, the sample does not contain exam scores for all the students enrolled because some students decided not to take part in the exam. Suppose that students at your university are less motivated – an unobserved variable – and that motivated students perform better at exams and are more likely to participate in exams. This situation is illustrated in Figure 1(b). In reality, there is no difference between your students and those at other universities (the dashed line is horizontal) although comparing the mean exam scores would falsely suggest that your students performed better. As always, the sample selection bias arises in this case because an unmeasured variable is correlated with the explanatory variable (your students are less motivated) and because this unmeasured variable is correlated with both the selection and the outcome (motivated students are more likely to participate in exams and perform better in exams).

The problem of causal inference

It is well-known that correlation does not imply causation. For example, there may be a correlation between going to bed with your shoes on and waking up with a headache, but this does not mean that a headache can be cured by removing your shoes. Contrary to what is sometimes thought, this problem of causal inference cannot be fixed by estimating a regression model rather than calculating a correlation coefficient. For example, if we use data on a number of fires to regress the damage of a fire on the number of firefighters involved, one would probably find a "significant" positive "effect". Again, this by no means implies that the best way to reduce fire damage is to send out less firefighters.

How, then, can a causal effect be demonstrated? Let us take up the example of returns to education again. It is hard to establish a causal relation between education and earning because the challenge is to demonstrate that education *alone* resulted in greater earnings (Gertler et al., 2011). The causal effect of education on earnings can be defined as the difference between the earnings of a high educated person and the earnings of the same person if he or she were low-educated. This way we would be certain that no confounding factors are influencing the difference in earnings. Unfortunately, it is impossible to measure the same person in two different educational backgrounds. It is relatively easy to measure the earnings of high educated persons. The challenge is to come up with a credible counterfactual, i.e. what would their earnings be had they been low-educated?

One method to come up with a counterfactual and to estimate the effect of a treatment in general is to compare the outcome before (control) and after (treated) the treatment. In the example of the returns to educations this would require to randomly select a group of people, to measure their wages when they have a low educational level, to then educate them and see how their subsequent wages compare to their initial wages. It is clear that such a design is difficult or even impossible to bring into practice. Moreover, bias may arise in before-and-after designs when other factors related to earnings are not constant over time. For example, the mere fact that the people are required to work before the treatment, changes their experience levels and their career history, which may affect the hiring decisions of employers after the treatment.

Another method to construct a counterfactual is to do a with-and-without comparison using two subsamples. However, estimating a treatment effect by subtracting the mean outcome in a control group from the mean outcome in a treated group, produces bias if the reasons why an individual is selected into the treated group also influence the outcome (selection bias). For example, the difference in earnings between high educated and low-educated people would be a biased estimate of the causal effect of education when students in higher education score higher on 'ability' or have richer parents than their peers who do not complete their education if ability or having rich parents increases earnings. In that case a spurious (apparent) correlation between education and earnings will arise in the sample data even when there is no causal effect of education on earnings. The best way for researchers to avoid selection bias is to use experimental designs (Heckman & Smith, 1995). In experiments the individuals are randomly assigned to the control and treated groups so that the reasons why an individual is selected into the treated group cannot influence the outcome (no selection bias). This property makes the experimental design increasingly popular among education researchers (Angrist, 2004). However, in many cases an experimental design is not feasible. Angrist and Pischke (2008) give the excellent advise that, even when an experiment is practically impossible and purely hypothetical, it is good practice to think about the 'ideal experiment in a world of no budgetary or normative constraints' that could be used to capture the causal effect of interest: "*If you can't devise an experiment that answers your question in a world where anything goes, then the odds of generating useful results with a modest budget and non-experimental survey data seem pretty slim. The description of an ideal experiment also helps you formulate causal questions precisely. The mechanics of an ideal experiment highlight the forces you'd like to manipulate and the factors you'd like to hold constant.*" In the example of the returns to education, our ideal experiment – barring one or two ethical issues – would be to randomly assign people to a control group that receives no education and a treatment group that does. Such an experiment is very hard to implement in practice, so we have to resort to the second-best option of using observational data and econometric techniques to counter potential selection bias as much as possible.

One of those econometric techniques is Heckman's sample selection model, which will be discussed in the next paragraph. There are alternative techniques, such as matching methods which rely on observed characteristics to construct a comparison group by identifying for every possible observation under treatment a non-treatment observation that has the most similar characteristics. The main limitation of this approach is that, very much like OLS regressions controlling for observables, bias caused by unobservables cannot be ruled out. Another technique is the use of instrumental variables, which requires variables that are correlated with the explanatory variables of interest but not with the outcome. A seminal article on the returns to education by Angrist and Krueger (1991) used variations in the quarter of birth among children as an instrument because this variation should not causally influence earnings, while it can be expected to be correlated with education because the quarter of birth determines to which class children are assigned and because school attendance in the US is compulsory until the age of 16. For a discussion on these techniques and related ones such as difference-in-differences and regression discontinuity designs – as well as an excellent introduction to the problem of selection bias – the reader is referred to the open access textbooks on impact evaluation provided by the World Bank (Khander et al., 2010; Gertler et al., 2011). A more technical discussion of the same issues can be found in Blundell and Dias (2009).

Sample selection bias

To understand in what circumstances Heckman's sample selection model applies, it is useful to distinguish sample selection bias from selection bias in general. Sample selection bias is a type of selection bias that can arise when the outcome variable is not observed if some criterion with respect to a different variable is met (Breen, 1996). If the outcome variable is observable for all the cases in the population then selection bias may still be possible – as always: when the reasons why an individual is selected into the treated group also influence the outcome – but this is generally not considered to be sample selection bias. Another situation that is typically not denoted as sample selection bias is the situation where the outcome variable is not observed if some criterion with respect to the outcome variable itself is met. An example is a study of the effect of education on earnings based only on data for people who earn 2000 euro per month or more. The estimated effect based on such a 'truncated sample' will be biased. It is possible to estimate the effect in the full, untruncated population based only on the truncated sample – see Wooldridge (2012) on truncated regression – but again this is normally not called sample selection bias. The situation in which we only observe the variable of interest because of the outcome of a different variable is called incidental truncation, which is often used interchangeably with the term sample selection. An example of incidental truncation is a study of the effect of education on earnings based only on data for public sector workers. Heckman's sample selection model corrects for sample selection bias, i.e. for selection bias arising from incidental truncation. Starting with Maddala (1983), Heckman's original model was later extended to correct for selection bias not arising from incidental truncation. In that situation the model is usually referred to as the treatment effect model (Greene, 2003), although it is similar to the sample selection model. Consider this example of an education research problem for which the treatment effect model would be appropriate. At our university first year business students have the option to take 4 hours of mathematics per week rather than the 2 hours per week in the regular program, but both groups of students must take the same exam and the end of the semester. We consistently find that the students taking 4 hours of mathematics have *lower* passing rates than students who only take 2 hours of mathematics. Could it be that the additional lectures on mathematics create that much confusion in the heads of the poor students that the additional classes negatively affect their exam performance? Although we are not sure whether the true causal effect of the additional classes is greater than zero or exactly zero, we doubt that it is less than zero. Most probably this is a case of selection bias because the weaker students are more likely to self-select into the group taking 4 hours of class per week. This is not a case of sample selection bias because we observe the outcome (to pass or not for the course) for all students. So the treatment effects model would be appropriate to study the causal relation of additional maths classes on student performance, rather than the Heckman sample selection model.

Incidental truncation or sample selection does not always lead to bias. It is important to know under which conditions sample selection bias arises in order to understand the problem one is trying to correct. Let us again take the example of the effect of education on female earnings. Women with high levels of education are more likely to enter the labour force, so the researcher will see a sample of educated women. Sartori (2003) rightly emphasizes that this non-random aspect of the sample is what is commonly *misunderstood* to be the problem of "selection bias". The fact that high educated women are more likely to be selected into the sample does not in itself bias the estimation. A sample can be selective (non-random) without producing biased or inconsistent estimates. This is the case when the incidental truncation of the sample is based on the explanatory variables that are included in the model. Figure 2(a) illustrates this important point using randomly generated data for a dependent variable y (think 'earnings') and one explanatory variable x_1 (think 'years of schooling'). Suppose that the outcome variable y is not observed if the variable x_1 is less than some cut-off c: only the observations to the right of c are observed. Since y is not observed when some criterion with respect to another variable (x_1) is met, this is a situation of incidental truncation. The grey dashed line in Figure 2 is the fit line based on the full population, including the unobserved cases. The black line shows the fit line using the selected sample only. The fit lines in the selected sample and the total population are very similar, illustrating that no bias arises when only the selected sample is used to estimate the effect of x_1. Figure 2(b) illustrates the same point for a multivariate model: incidental truncation on x_1 in this example does not bias the coefficient of another explanatory variable x_2. Achen (1986) notes that this result justifies stratified sampling. Researchers often oversample certain subgroups in a population, thereby creating a non-representative sample. This does not pose a problem if subgroup memberships are controlled for in subsequent regressions because the truncation is then based on independent variables.

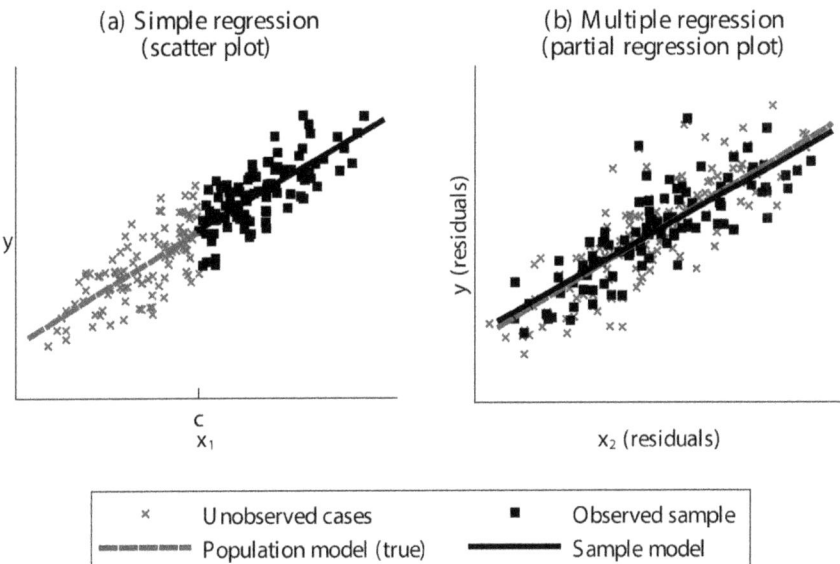

Note: graphs based on randomly generated data. The observed sample (n=100) and the unobserved cases (n=100) in both graphs are the same. The truncation for the observed sample was based on x1. The result in (b) does not follow from uncorrelated independent variables (the correlation between x1 and x2 was made r=.7).

Figure 2-2 Incidental truncation based on independent variables does not produce bias

So in which cases does incidental truncation lead to bias? There are two necessary conditions for sample selection bias to occur in the estimation of the effect of an explanatory variable on an outcome of interest:
    1. Unobserved variables influence both the outcome of interest and the probability of selection into the sample.
    2. The probability of selection into the sample is correlated with the explanatory variable.

In the example of sample selection bias in the estimation of the effect of education of earnings, the first condition requires that ability (an unobserved variable) is correlated with both earnings (the outcome of interest) and being in the labour force (selection into the sample). This condition implies incidental truncation based on an unobserved variable. The second condition requires that being in the labour force (selection into the sample) is correlated with education (the explanatory variable). There is no bias if the explanatory variable is uncorrelated with sample selection because, as we will discuss in the next paragraph, sample selection bias can be regarded as a form of omitted variable bias and an omitted variable only produces bias in the coefficient of a variable it is correlated with. For example, a regression of earnings on gender in which a variable measuring the number of working hours per week is omitted, produces bias in the gender coefficient because women on average work less hours per week than men so that the effect of working hours on earnings will be erroneously attributed to gender in the misspecified model. For similar reasons, failing to control for sample selectivity will lead to bias in the coefficient estimates of the included variables if these explanatory variables are correlated with sample selectivity so that the effect of sample selectivity will be erroneously attributed to the included variables.

3. Heckman's sample selection model

In this paragraph we try to clarify the intuition behind the Heckman sample selection model. In the example of the effect of education on female earnings, sample selection bias arises because only the earnings of women in the labour force are observed. Heckman showed that it is possible to get consistent estimates of the effect of education on earnings using the earnings data of a sample of employed women only. This was an extremely important result, for which Heckman was awarded the nobel prize in economics. The intuition behind Heckman's method is quite simple, which is the case for many great ideas. The reader interested in an introduction to the mathematical technicalities behind the model is referred to Greene (2003) or Wooldridge (2012).

From the example of the returns to education in Figure 1(a), we concluded that sample selection bias results from the fact that high educated women are more likely to be selected into the sample and that those low-educated who do work score relatively well on unobserved characteristics like ability. Using a sample of employed women only would thus tend to underestimate the returns to education. Note that this bias would not occur if we were somehow able to compare the earnings of high educated women to the earnings of low-educated women *who are equally likely of being selected into the sample*. To remove the sample selection bias we would need to estimate the effect of education on earnings holding constant the probability of selection into the sample. Holding a factor constant is easy to do in a multivariate regression framework because regression coefficients measure the effect of an explanatory variable ceteris paribus, i.e. holding all the other included variables constant. All that is required is the inclusion of that factor into the model as an additional control variable. The sample selection model does exactly that: first it estimates the probability of selection into the sample for each observation and then the model of interest is estimated by adding the selection probabilities from the first step as an additional control variable. The important conclusion is that sample selection bias arises because a relevant variable – i.e. the probability of selection into the sample – is omitted from the regression model. It is well known that omitting a relevant variable is the greatest source of bias in econometrics. Using an earlier example: a regression estimate of the effect of going to bed with your shoes on at night on the probability to wake up with a headache in the morning, is biased because the relevant variable alcohol consumption is not controlled for. To estimate the true effect of going to bed with your shoes on at night it is necessary to compare treated and control groups of people with the same level of alcohol consumption Similarly, to estimate the true effect of education on earnings it is necessary to compare treated and control groups of people with the same probability of selection into the sample. Sample selection bias can thus be regarded as a type of omitted variable bias. OLS is biased because the model is misspecified, i.e. not all the relevant explanatory variables are included. Heckman's (1979) famous article developing this idea was aptly titled *"Sample selection bias as a specification error"*.

In practice the estimation of the sample selection model involves two steps. The first step is to estimate the probability of selection into the sample for each case. These probabilities are never directly observed because we only observe a binary variable indicating whether the case is included in the sample (1) or not (0). It is possible to obtain estimates of the selection probabilities by first estimating a binary regression model (probit) with the selection variable as the dependent variable and subsequently using this model to calculate predicted probabilities for each case. To estimate this so-called 'selection equation' (the probit model), data are required on both selected and unselected cases. In the example of the effect of education on female earnings: although information on earnings may be lacking for those outside the employed labour force, data on the factors determining employment are needed for both the employed and the non-employed. The practical implication is that a sample selection model requires data about the out-group as well. The second step of Heckman's two-step method to correct for sample selection bias, is to include the predicted selection probabilities from the first step as an additional variable in the outcome equation. In the example of the returns to education, the predicted employment probabilities are added to the regression model in which earnings are the dependent variable. For technical reasons, it is not the predicted probabilities themselves that are included, but the so-called Inverse Mills Ratios (IMR), which are inversely related to the predicted selection probabilities. Intuitively, the IMR should be understood as the probability of not being selected into the sample (strictly speaking the IMR are not probabilities because they are not limited between 0 and 1). In a regression model of earnings, the coefficient of the IMR is usually negative because the higher the probability of *not* being selected into the labour force, the lower the predicted earnings.

Although in principle Heckman's model is an appealing method to correct for potential sample selection bias, there are a number of difficulties in practice which have attracted some criticism (Puhani, 2000). In practice, the outcome and selection equations often have many independent variables in common – in some cases even the exact same set of variables is used. The IMR is then a function of the explanatory variables in the outcome equation, resulting in high collinearity in the second step of the Heckman procedure. Let us consider once again the example of the effect of education on female earnings. Suppose only the variable education is used to model the selection into employment (the probit model), then the resulting predicted employment probabilities and the accompanying IMR will be a function of education. The second step would be the estimation of an earnings function with the education variable and the IMR as independents. Because education and the IMR will be highly correlated, OLS will have difficulties in separating the effects on sample selection versus education. In such a situation, small alterations in the data produce large variations in the estimated coefficients. The estimated coefficients will be highly unstable and thus not robust.

4. The sample selection model in educational research

Bibliometric analysis and literature review

We carried out a systematic literature review (Torraco, 2005) in order to investigate the use of the Heckman sample selection model in educational research. In order to select our sample of articles to be studied, we first selected journals using the 2013 Journal Citation Reports database of ISI Web of Knowledge. We included in our sample the only journal in this database that is ranked in both the subject category 'economics' and the category 'education and educational research': the *Economics of Education Review* (EER).[4] Between the launching of the EER in 1981 and the time of this study in the summer of 2014, 1571 full articles were published in this journal. An archive search on the journal's webpage shows that 386 articles (25% of all articles) explicitly discuss sample selection bias in its full text.[5] 54 articles (14% of all articles discussing selection bias) explicitly discuss the Heckman sample selection model.[6] These 54 articles form our sample for the systematic literature review we discuss below.

A closer reading showed that only 43 of these articles actually estimated a Heckman model. The remaining 11 articles either refer to the use of Heckman models in their literature review or the authors argue that sample selection bias is not likely to pose a problem so that a Heckman correction is not needed (e.g. Hill, 1989). In some instances the authors use different methods, for example an instrumental variables approach to estimate the returns to education of which the results are then compared to other results in the literature coming from Heckman approaches (Bedi & Gaston, 1999). An interesting example of an article that in fact does not estimate a Heckman model but which discusses the sample selection problem and the Heckman model at length, is Glick and Sahn's (2000) study on the effects of family characteristics on the schooling of 13-18 year olds in West-Africa. The authors realize that selection bias may be present because they only have data on children living with their parents, while a very large percentage (up to 50%!) of these children in the country they study (Guinea) live away from their parents because of traditions of child fostering and early marriage of girls. The authors admit that sample selection may produce bias, for example because unobserved parental preferences could be correlated with both the selection into the sample (children living with their parents)

---

[4] The *Journal of Economic Education* is also ranked in both categories, but we decided not to include this journal in our sample because it is about economic education rather than the economics of education.

[5] We searched for full articles on: JOURNAL-NAME("economics of education review") AND Full-Text ("selection bias" OR "selectivity bias" OR "heckman correction" OR "heckit" OR "sample selection model" OR "mills ratio").

[6] We searched for full articles on: JOURNAL-NAME("economics of education review") AND Full-Text ("heckman correction" OR "heckit" OR "sample selection model" OR "mills ratio").

and the outcome variable (schooling). By giving such examples of unobservables and thereby clarifying the potential channel for selection bias, this article is truly exemplary because most of the articles we studied refrain from doing this (we return to this point later). However, the authors do not carry out a Heckman correction, most probably because they have no information about children living away from their parents so that a selection equation cannot be estimated. Interestingly, the authors do provide an extensive mathematical treatment of the Heckman sample selection model. One might think that this is merely done to please reviewers in the publication process, but the authors actually use the formulated model to extensively reflect on the likely size and direction of the potential bias in each of the explanatory variables in their model (*Ibid.*, footnotes 25 and 28). For example, they deduce that their estimate of the effect of household income on schooling is probably underestimated in their analysis (because children in low income households are more likely to live away from their parents and those children of low income households who do live with their parents, probably have parental preferences which are positively correlated with schooling – the situation is analogous to the bias in the example in Figure 1(a)). This reflection on the likely direction of potential sample selection bias is an exemplary practice which we recommend not just for studies that for some technical reason are unable to estimate a Heckman model. Thinking about the likely direction of bias and making explicit the potential channels by which this bias arises *in the concrete research setting* at hand and *before* the empirical results are presented, not only helps the reader but – more importantly – provides a basic plausibility check. Thinking about the expected signs of coefficients is a standard recommendation in econometrics textbooks because "wrong signs" can point to problems with the model (Wooldridge, 2012) such as misspecification or collinearity, but for some reason this practice is rarely applied when it comes to Heckman models.

In the sample of 43 articles in which a Heckman model is applied, we investigated which research topics are studied, how the problem of sample selection bias is framed and how the results of the heckit models are presented and interpreted. Figure 3 summarizes the quantitative results of this analysis. Almost half of the articles studied (47% or 20 out of a total of 43 articles) deal with the topic of returns to education and the estimation of skill premia. This should be no surprise because it is for this application that James Heckman originally developed his sample selection model. The non-random selection into employment is the classical example for Heckman's model, which makes the model difficult to ignore for scholars investigating the effect of education on earnings. Most of the other articles (16 out of 43, i.e. 37%) investigate the determinants of student test scores and learning performance. In these articles educational variables play the role of dependent variables, as opposed to the literature on skill premia where education is an explanatory variable.

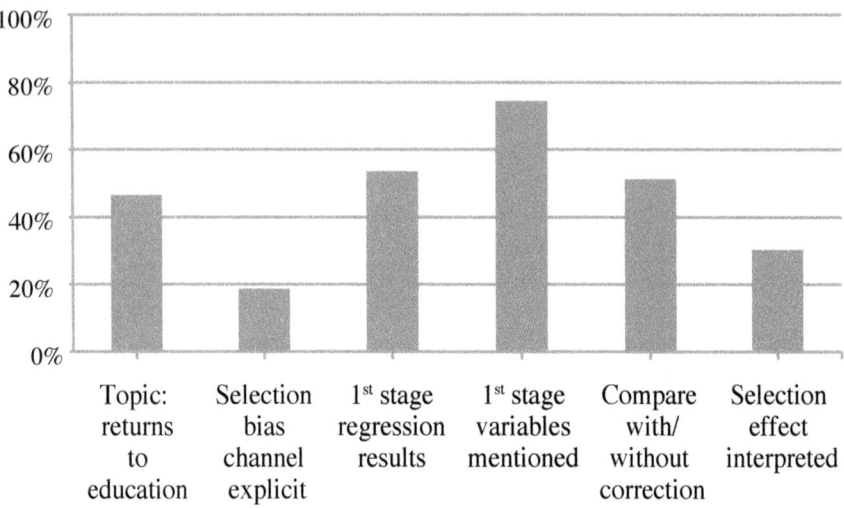

Figure 2-3 Sample characteristics of journal articles using heckit models in educational research (N=43)

We find only 8 articles in our sample (19%) in which the selection bias channel is made explicit by explaining, in the concrete research setting at hand, how bias could arise in the estimated effect of the explanatory variable of interest because of sample selectivity. Most articles limit their discussion about the potential sources of selection bias to general and abstract statements such as *"The outcome variable is only observed for a part of the population. In this case, the OLS method provides biased estimations. This selection bias can be treated through the Heckman selection model".*[7] We looked for a concrete description – using an example of an unobserved variable – of how sample selection bias could arise and in what direction the bias is likely to be. Examples of good practices in this regard are Grubb (1993), McHenry (2011) and Glick and Sahn (2000), i.e. the earlier discussed study on schooling in West-Africa. Although we admit that in studies about the returns to education, the need to make the selection bias channel explicit is less urgent because the channel in this case is well-known, we find the general lack of clarity about potential selection bias channels a major shortcoming in the literature on applied Heckman models. This lack of clarity is also evident from the methodology sections in some of the articles in our sample. For example, one author working on the returns to education explains: *"The problem is that the unobserved wage offers of those not working are probably lower than those for persons in the sample. To correct for this we use Heckman's technique. See Heckman (1979) for a discussion of this problem"*. As stated before, the non-random aspect of the sample is what is commonly misunderstood to be the problem of "selection bias" (Sartori, 2003), but it does not in itself bias the estimation of an effect (in paragraph 2 we discussed

---

[7] We do not provide references for this citation and some citations below. The exact sources of these citations are not important because similar examples abound in the literature. Note that, strictly speaking, the stated citation is wrong because truncation not always produces bias as was argued earlier in this chapter.

this issue at length). Another author working on the returns to education writes: *"… this also introduces a bias in our estimates, since our sample is not representative of the whole population. This problem – of sample selection bias – can be solved and estimates with desirable asymptotic properties (consistency) can be obtained using a procedure described in Heckman (1979)".* Although these cited examples are not strictly wrong, they are not clarifying because they do not refer to the essential role of unmeasured variables in sample selection bias. In one article we encountered an explanation for sample selection bias arising from selection based on independent variables, which – as we illustrated in Figure 2 – does not produce bias. The authors argue that *"…unemployment is concentrated especially among low-skill workers. This might tend estimates of earnings functions to be affected by sample selection, causing, in turn, an upward bias in the returns to education. In other words, the sample of paid workers could include a relatively larger share of skilled individuals compared to the population. To test for this hypothesis, we implement the Heckman (1979) correction model".* The fact that skilled individuals are overrepresented in the sample is an example of selection based on education, which does not in itself lead to bias in the estimated effect of education on earnings. Moreover, the likely direction of sample selection bias in this case would be downward – not upward – because those low-skilled workers who are employed most probably have characteristics that increase their wages compared to the unemployed low-skilled (see Figure 1(a)).

A majority of the articles in our sample (54%) provides the coefficient estimates of the selection equation, i.e. the first stage probit model. Some articles do not present the coefficient estimates but list in the text which explanatory variables were included in the selection equation, so that in 74% of the articles the included explanatory variables are mentioned. This is important not just for purposes of replication, but also to judge the validity of the results (see our earlier discussion on collinearity in the Heckman model). Only half of the articles in the sample (51%) present and compare the results of the outcome equation with a correction for selectivity and without such a correction. Such a comparison is useful because it shows the extent of the selection bias and because it allows both the researcher and the reader to judge the plausibility of the findings. For example, in a conventional study about the returns to education we would expect the effect of education on earnings to be greater after selectivity correction than before such a correction: if the results point the other way, then the researcher should discuss whether the source of this result is the nature of the topic that is being studied (there may be reasons why in some particular settings the selection effect works the other way) or the specification used in the model.

Finally, we find that in only 13 articles (30%) the estimated coefficient of the selectivity term in the outcome model (the IMR) is discussed in a concrete manner by correctly interpreting the sign of the estimated coefficient. In many cases the estimated coefficient is not included in the tables presenting the results and, if it is included, the discussion is often limited to general statements such as *"The selectivity factor coefficient is highly significant. This means that being an employee has a significant impact on earnings".* In general, the coefficient of the selection term is the effect, ceteris paribus, on the outcome of interest when the IMR increases by one unit. Because the IMR are inversely related to the predicted selection probabilities, the sign of the estimated coefficient of the selection term can be interpreted as the effect of not being selected into the sample on the outcome variable. In conventional studies about the returns to education we would expect this coefficient to be negative because the probability of not being employed can, ceteris paribus, be expected to be negatively correlated with potential earnings (or said differently: the expected effect of being in employment on potential earnings is positive). In 3 articles in our sample (7%) the interpretation of the estimated IMR coefficient was plainly wrong. Most articles do not discuss the estimated coefficient and thus miss the opportunity to discuss the selection effects. Some examples in the field of earnings functions are Kim (2001), who finds a positive coefficient, and Dabos and Psacharopoulos (1991), who find a negative coefficient in one specification and a positive coefficient in another specification. An example among the 13 articles that do interpret the sign of the estimated coefficient of the selectivity term is Kimmel (1997) who estimates an earnings function and concludes *"the sample selection correction term is significantly negative for both Blacks and Whites in both specifications, implying a negative correlation between unobservables in the labour force participation and wage equations. In other words, something unobserved that decreases one's chances of working will also tend to reduce one's wage."*

Case studies

This paragraph contains a more in-depth discussion of two topics from the sample of 43 EER articles that apply a heckit model in educational research. In selecting the topics, we looked for articles that apply the Heckman model to an original question and that are interesting from a methodological point of view.

a) The effect of teacher experience on student performance

Winters et al. (2012) study the effect of teacher characteristics on student performance. They are particularly interested in the effect of teacher experience (in years) on student test scores. Interestingly, the authors argue that conventional OLS estimates of this effect could be biased because of sample selection among teachers. There is substantial attrition from the teaching profession, particularly in the first years after entering the classroom, and this attrition is almost certainly non-random. Suppose that the more "able" (an unobserved variable) teachers are more likely to stay in the profession (to be selected in the sample) and suppose that these more able teachers are more efficient in terms of increasing their student's test scores (the outcome variable), then OLS would tend to overestimate the effect of teacher experience on student performance: an apparent positive effect of teacher experience might simply be caused by the fact that the group of the more experienced teachers is a highly selective group of "able" teachers because their less able colleagues dropped out of the profession over the years. The authors estimate a first stage probit model for selection into the teaching profession (non-attrition) and add the resulting IMR to models of student test scores on math and reading proficiency. They compare the estimated effects with and without correcting for selection bias and are able to show that conventional OLS estimates are indeed biased upwards (but the differences are small and not always significant so that the authors conclude that failure to account for selection bias does not appear to severely hamper estimation).

b) Determinants of learning gains

The best studies about the determinants of learning performance compare test results after an instruction phase (post) to the test results for the same students before the instruction (pre). Investigating learning gains has the advantage of eliminating much of the potential omitted variable bias that would be present if only post-scores would be analysed. A disadvantage is that some students that take part in the pre-test may drop out and not participate in the post-test. Unobserved characteristics such as "ability" or "motivation" are likely to be positively correlated with both taking the post-test (selection into the sample) and higher learning gains (the outcome). If these unobserved variables are correlated with an explanatory variable in the study, then OLS would attribute the selectivity effect to this explanatory variable resulting in sample selection bias. Two studies in our sample apply the Heckman model to correct for this potential bias: one study about learning gains of 12 year-olds in rural Guatemala (Marshall, 2009) and one about learning gains among adult learners in Nicaragua (Handa et al., 2009). In both studies a first stage probit model is estimated for the probability of participating in both the pre- and post-tests (selection into the sample) and the resulting IMR are added to the outcome equation of learning gains. Interestingly, Handa et al. include the distance to the testing centre in the probit model as it is reasonable to assume that it will affect the probability of attending the second test, but itself should not affect learning. Marshall adds measures of the mother's work participation to the probit model. This is not so obvious because one could ask why these measures are to be excluded from the outcome equation, but the author argues that this *"identification strategy is supported empirically by the significance of the instrument set in the selection equation and the lack of power of these same variables in the achievement production functions"*. Both studies tend to find negative coefficients for the selection term, implying that the higher the probability of dropping out between both tests, the lower the predicted learning gains (which is a plausible result). Marshall correctly interprets this result as *"a negative effect on average achievement when the school does a better job of retaining students"*. Unfortunately, neither of both studies compares the selectivity corrected results with conventional OLS estimates. In the Guatemalan case this could have been illuminating because the author is particularly interested in explaining the poor study performance of indigenous students, which is a pressing social question in contemporary Guatemalan society. Comparing the effect of indigenous roots on study performance between OLS and selectivity corrected estimates could have shed more light on the role of selectivity in the observed performance of this group.

5. Conclusion

Sample selection bias is an issue in many educational research topics. It was in his seminal study about the effects of education on earnings that James Heckman developed the sample selection model, which in some cases can be used to correct for this type of bias. However, sample selection bias is not confined to this classical case, but also affects estimates of causal relations in which educational variables are the dependent variable. This chapter discussed sources of sample selection bias in analyses ranging from student test-score differences across universities to schooling in West-Africa and the effects of teachers dropping out of the teaching profession.

A systematic review of the literature on the use of the Heckman sample selection model in education research issues indicates that the model provides a powerful tool for addressing sample selectivity. Education economists now apply the Heckman model to a much broader array of questions than just the classical case of returns to education. However, we feel that there are weaknesses in the way the Heckman model is applied in practice. The literature review indicates that only about 20 percent of the journal articles applying a heckit model, make the selection bias channel explicit by explaining how sample selection bias could arise in the concrete research setting at hand. We recommend that researchers, before presenting selectivity corrected results, reflect on the direction the sample selection bias is likely to have. We cited exemplary studies in this regard. We also recommend that researchers compare the results of the outcome equation with a correction for selectivity and without such a correction in order to clarify the extent of the selection bias. Our final recommendation is for researchers to present the coefficient of the selection term and to discuss the direction of the selection effect.

The main weakness of the Heckman approach, apart from the important issue of finding strong instruments to be included in the selection equation, is the lack of clarity that sometimes surrounds the method. As economists and educational researchers increasingly gear towards experimental designs, new and stronger evidence may appear that re-adjusts previous findings. The Heckman model essentially tries to correct for potential bias, whereas an experimental designs avoids the bias in the first place. However, for many issues, including many educational research issues, experiments are simply not feasible and observational data is then the best we have. Heckman's sample selection model is then a powerful framework for reflecting on and correcting for sample selection bias.

References

Achen, C. H. (1986). *The statistical analysis of quasi-experiments*. Berkeley: University of California Press.

Angrist (2004): "American Education Research Changes Track,"*Oxford Review of Economic Policy, 20*, 198-212.

Angrist, J. D., & Krueger, A. B. (1991). Does Compulsory School Attendance Affect Schooling and Earnings? *Quarterly Journal of Economics, 106(4)*, 979-1014.

Angrist, J. D., & Pischke, J. S. (2008). *Mostly harmless econometrics: An empiricist's companion*. Princeton university press.

Bedi, A. S., & Gaston, N. (1999). Using variation in schooling availability to estimate educational returns for Honduras. *Economics of Education Review, 18(1)*, 107-116.

Blundell, R., & Dias, M. C. (2009). Alternative approaches to evaluation in empirical microeconomics. *Journal of Human Resources, 44(3)*, 565-640.

Breen, R. (1996). *Regression models: Censored, sample selected, or truncated data*. Quantitative applications in the social sciences, No. 111. Sage.

Dabos, M., & Psacharopoulos, G. (1991). An analysis of the sources of earnings variation among Brazilian males. *Economics of Education Review, 10(4)*, 359-377.

Glick, P., & Sahn, D. E. (2000). Schooling of girls and boys in a West African country: the effects of parental education, income, and household structure. *Economics of education review, 19(1)*, 63-87.

Greene, W. H. (2003). *Econometric analysis*. Upper Saddle River, NJ.

Grubb, W. N. (1993). Further tests of screening on education and observed ability. *Economics of Education Review, 12(2)*, 125-136.

Handa, S., Pineda, H., Esquivel, Y., Lopez, B., Gurdian, N. V., & Regalia, F. (2009). Non-formal basic education as a development priority: Evidence from Nicaragua. *Economics of Education Review, 28(4)*, 512-522.

Heckman, J. J. (1979). Sample selection bias as a specification error. *Econometrica: Journal of the econometric society*, 153-161.

Heckman, J. J., & Smith, J. A. (1995). Assessing the case for social experiments. *Journal of Economic Perspectives*, 85-110.

Hill, E. T. (1989). Postsecondary technical education, performance and employee development: A survey of employers. *Economics of Education Review, 8(4)*, 323-333.

Kim, H. K. (2001). Is there a crowding-out effect between school expenditure and mother's child care time?. *Economics of Education Review, 20(1)*, 71-80.

Kimmel, J. (1997). Rural wages and returns to education: Differences between whites, blacks, and American Indians. *Economics of Education Review, 16(1)*, 81-96.

Maddala, G. S. (1983). *Limited-dependent and qualitative variables in econometrics*. Cambridge university press.

Marshall, J. H. (2009). School quality and learning gains in rural Guatemala. *Economics of Education Review, 28(2)*, 207-216.

McHenry, P. (2011). The effect of school inputs on labor market returns that account for selective migration. *Economics of Education Review, 30(1)*, 39-54.

Puhani, P. (2000). The Heckman correction for sample selection and its critique. *Journal of Economic Surveys, 14(1)*, 53-68.

Sartori, A. E. (2003). An Estimator for Some Binary-Outcome Selection Models Without Exclusion Restrictions. *Political Analysis, 11(2)*, 111-138.

Torraco, R. J. (2005). Writing integrative literature reviews: Guidelines and examples. *Human Resource Development Review, 4(3)*, 356-367.

Winters, M. A., Dixon, B. L., & Greene, J. P. (2012). Observed characteristics and teacher quality: Impacts of sample selection on a value added model. *Economics of Education Review, 31(1)*, 19-32.

Wooldridge, J. (2012). *Introductory econometrics: A modern approach*. Cengage Learning.

CHAPTER 3

The Causal Effect of Single-Sex Education versus Coeducation on Motivation and Educational Attainments. Evidence from a Randomized Experiment in Secondary Education[1]

Kristof De Witte[2*], *Oliver Holz* [*]

1. Introduction

Mixed-sex education, also known as coeducation, has been extensively studied during the last century. 3-1 presents a density distribution of book counts where 'coeducation' has been recorded as a proportion of all Google-digitized books in English from 1880 until 2008. The graph starts around the time that the 'Welsh Intermediate Education Act' in 1889 led to the foundation of a considerable number of new coeducational secondary day-schools in Wales. Its positive effects inspired various other European countries as the Netherlands, Norway, Sweden and Denmark. In Norway, coeducation was adapted by law in 1896. Despite these early initiatives, in the beginning of the 20th century, there was still large resistance against coeducation. Catholics argued that it would raise debauchery and create an unhealthy competition between sexes. This view was further strengthened by the opinion that boys and girls were considered to have different purposes to fulfill. Most Catholic secondary schools remained single-sex institutions until 1940s.

Due to the second World War there was a radical shift in gender roles. Labor force participation of women increased such that educational opportunities were increasingly considered to be equal. After 1940 coeducation was generally accepted in primary and secondary education (for an excellent overview, see Rury, 2008).

Still after years of practicing coeducation, the debate remerged in the 1970s. Academic research suggested higher levels of female academic achievement in single-sex institutions compared to mixed-sex educational institutions (e.g. Finn, 1980; Finn et al.,

---
[1] We would like to thank participants of the 2014 Education and Gender Conference at Izmir University of Economics, Bart van Hempen, Trui De Vos, Carla Cosyns, Ingrid De Hanscutter, and Jeroen Schouppe for valuable comments and the help with the data collection.
[2] Maastricht University; TIER, Faculty of Humanities and Sciences; PO Box 616, 6200MD Maastricht (the Netherlands); T +31433884458; k.dewitte@maastrichtuniversity.nl
[*] Katholieke Universiteit Leuven (KU Leuven); Leuven Economics of Education Research, Faculty of Business and Economics; Naamsestraat 69, 3000 Leuven (Belgium); Kristof.dewitte@kuleuven.be.

1979; Ormerod, 1973). In 1992, the American Association of University Women triggered the debate about coeducation by their report 'How Schools Shortchange Girls'. Their report suggests that women are ignored in class discussions and are subject to threats of sexual harassment. Following this report, there were experiments with single-sex education. While before the 21th century the social position and academic achievement of women played a central role in the coeducation debate, since 2000 it became clear that boys are underperforming girls (e.g., Alloway and Gilbert, 1997; Jackson, 2002; Jha and Kelleher, 2006; Whitmire, 2010). Besides differences in learning style and curriculum (Coffield et al., 2004), the lack of male teachers (Dee, 2005) and gender stereotypes (Guiso et al., 2008), various researchers point to coeducation as the origin of this underperformance (e.g. Houtte, 2004; Warrington and Younger, 2003).

Source: Google Books Ngram Viewer (2014). Graph indicates the density of book counts where coeducation have been recorded as a proportion of all Google digitized books in English from 1880 to 2008

Figure 3-1 Coeducation in the literature

The fact that boys are underperforming can be observed from international studies. The following overview lists some of the studies carried out in the last few years:

1. PISA-Study (Programme for International Student Assessment)

The survey aims 15-year-olds in terms of their skills in reading, mathematics and natural sciences. For this purpose, an appropriate research design was developed under the auspices of the OECD. With regard to differences between girls and boys generally two main results can be summed up:
- The difference between the tested boys and girls in reading and mathematical literacy is particularly clear (in terms of reading capability gender differences are significant).
- The difference in gender for mathematical literacy in 2012 was larger than that of the test phase in 2003.

2. TIMSS (Trends in Mathematics and Science Study)

The international comparative Study, TIMSS is carried out since 1995, in a rhythm of every 4 years by the International Association for the Evaluation of Educational Achievement (IEA). It examines mathematics and science performances in primary and secondary education. Since 2003, the acronym TIMSS stands for Trends in International Mathematics and Science Study.

In regard to the results, it can be stated in summary, that there is no unified picture what the mathematical performance is concerned. Especially in terms of performance weaker countries, a significant advantage in performance is observed for girls. In the countries of the European Union relevant gender differences are rarely observed.

The status of research on gender issues in the evaluation of academic performance is limited to date mostly to the mathematical-scientific part and is summarized by Nagy as follows: "The relationship between motivational attitudes and achievement differences in mathematics and natural sciences is well documented. Girls have less favourable attitudes than boys towards the education of mathematics and natural sciences, which are related to stereotyping in and towards the respective subject. There is evidence that favourable motivational attitudes towards mathematics and natural sciences are linked to didactic characteristics of teaching (...)."(Nagy 2009).

3. PIRLS (Progress in International Reading Literacy Study)

With PIRLS, the reading comprehension of students of the fourth grade is tested in an international comparison. PIRLS, as well as TIMSS, is conducted by the International Association for the Evaluation of Educational Achievement.

Comparing the results of girls and boys in their entirety, it can be concluded that with the exception of Luxembourg and Spain, girls statistically score significantly better in all participating countries than boys.

4. A further study on 'Gender Differences in Educational Outcomes: Study on the Measures Taken and the Current Situation in Europe' (European Commission 2009) had the initial idea to examine to what extent and in what ways gender inequality in educational attainment was an issue of concern in European countries. Although the situation has changed radically in the last decades regarding participation rates in education, gender differences persist in both attainment and choice of courses of study. It states that:

- The most pronounced gender difference in achievement is the advantage of girls in reading. On average, girls read more and enjoy reading more than boys.
- In mathematics, boys and girls have similar results in the fourth and eighth grade in most countries. The advantage of boys emerges in the later school years and is especially noticeable among students who attend the same teaching programmes and grades.
- Gender differences in science achievement are the smallest. Despite performing equally well as boys in most countries, girls tend to have a weaker self-concept in science than males, i.e., on average, girls had lower levels of belief in their science abilities than boys. Yet, both boys and girls are similarly interested in science; and there is no overall difference in boys' and girls' inclination to use science in future studies or jobs.
- Boys are more likely to be amongst the poorest performers in reading. In mathematics and science, there are no gender differences amongst low achievers in most countries.
- Gender is only one of the factors that affect achievement in various subject fields. Socio-economic status is a very strong factor; thus it is important to consider family background alongside gender when supporting children who are underachieving (European Commission 2009, p. 11).

As mentioned before, one of the solutions to reduce gender inequality is by making single sex groups. Given that making separate education groups for boys and girls is expensive and difficult to implement, given the significant impact of single-sex education on the education system and given the inconclusive evidence today, further research is necessary. After arguing the drawbacks of earlier literature, this paper provides experimental evidence from a large school in Flanders (the Dutch speaking region of Belgium). By randomly dividing students to single-sex and mixed-sex education groups, we can estimate the causal effect of coeducation on students' motivation and educational attainments. The evidence is obtained from both a quantitative analysis of survey and multiple choice data, as well as from a qualitative assessment by observational studies. We will answer the following research questions:

> Do students in single-sex groups outperform students in coeducational groups in terms of motivation and educational attainments?
> Are the effects of coeducation different for different age groups?

The remainder of this chapter is structured as follows. Section 2 discusses the inconclusive evidence from earlier literature, some didactical tools to reduce underperformance, as well as earlier shortcomings which might lead to biased inferences. Section 3 present the Flemish education system, while section 4 discusses the data and experiment. Section 5 and 6 outline the quantitative and qualitative analysis, respectively. We finally conclude and provide policy recommendations.

2. Literature review

Inconclusive evidence

The academic literature is inconclusive on whether the educational outcomes of boys and girls are influenced by mixed-sex education (Munns et al., 2012). Figure 3-2 provides a summary of literature on the effects of single-sex education (see also Munns et al. (2012) for a more extensive review). Focusing on educational achievement (the upper row of Figure 3-2), we observe studies with positive, as well as insignificant results of single-sex education. Regarding the classroom climate, the literature argues that single-sex classes have a better class atmosphere.

The underlying mechanisms which support the views on coeducation are diverse. It has been argued by Sukhnandan et al. (2000) and Younger and Warrington (2005) that single-sex education provides less distraction to both boys and girls. This argument is rooted in biological and social psychological theories. Lee, Marks and Byrd (1994) suggest that boys dominate in class groups such that they receive a disproportionally large share of the teacher's attention. This in turn would reduce girls' interest in Science-Technology-Engineering-Math (STEM – Sadker and Zittleman, 2009), as would it reduce their academic achievements (Shapka and Keating, 2003).

Park, Behram and Choi (2013) examine in a randomized experiment the causal effects of single-sex schools on college entrance and college exams. They observe that single-sex schools produce a higher percentage of graduates, even after controlling for observed heterogeneity. Similar observations have been made by Nagengast, Marsh and Hau (2013). Using a matching analysis they observe little evidence for positive effects of single-sex schooling on the outcomes in the final two years of high school. On the contrary, using the variation in single-sex education originating from an assignment algorithm, Jackson (2012) observed that most students do not perform better in single-sex schools. Also Van de Gaer et al. (2004) and Harker (2000) observed similar findings.

While the aforementioned papers focused on school outcomes, Sullivan, Joshi and Leonard (2010) examine the effects of single-sex schooling in the long run. They observe in terms of educational attainments that single-sex schooling is positive for girls at age 16, but neutral for boys, while both genders attain qualification in more gender-atypical subject areas due to single-sex schooling. The influence of single-sex education has also been studied with respect to choices for particular study programs. For example Cherney and Campbell (2011) observe that students from single-sex schools have more participation in physical sciences.

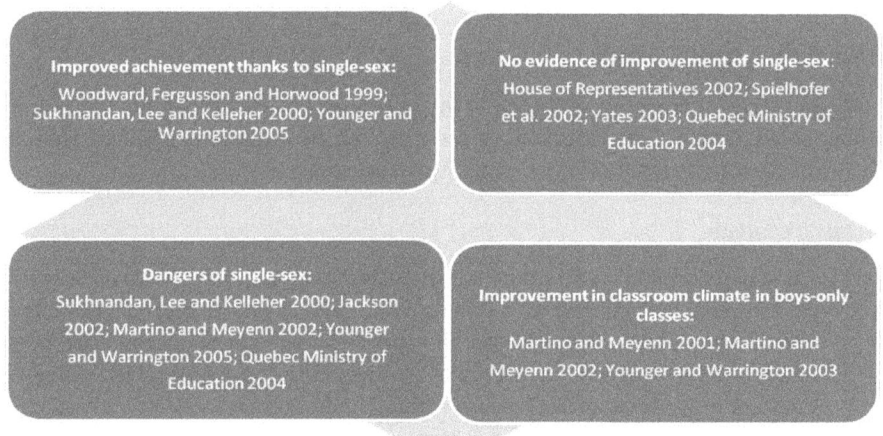

Figure 3-2 Earlier literature on single-sex education (adapted from Munns et al., 2012)

Didactics for gender-equitable education

The coeducational school as a sphere of social interaction is gender-dynamically charged. Girls and boys spend a weighty part of their time in the school's community. Until the entry into adolescence, both gender spheres often tend to be highly differentiated. Boys set themselves usually apart from girls and prefer to keep to themselves, where girls also prefer the presence of other girls. In this regard the learning processes that can be found in single-sex peer groups, is of great importance for gender education.

An important influence on the behaviour of girls and boys is attributed to the interaction with male and female teachers. The importance of gender and the charging of gender images are produced as well as reproduced by the participating teachers. Thus, the teachers are involved and instrumental in the success or failure of coeducational learning situations.

These featured comparative studies reflect different accents of gender differences. The accompanying question regarding the implementation of single-sex and coeducational classes is raised repeatedly.

Undoubtedly, the array of coeducational programmes for female and male students is one of the achievements of the educational policy of recent decades. Gender-appropriate and gender-sensitive teaching has received a new significance in the wake of these developments. It must be emphasized that in this context, coeducation is not only limited to the simultaneous teaching of boys and girls. Rather, co-education – as already pointed out higher above – is a conscious examination of gender specific prejudices. It is important to select learning contents that appeal to both girls and boys and to make lessons so that they meet the needs of girls and boys. In addition, it is important to create a climate of mutual attention and respect. Coeducation does not exclude the forming of nor teaching in homogeneous groups. "Teaching in gender homogeneous groups can contribute to an expansion of the behavioral and interest range of girls and boys. Therefore, it may be useful in connection to specific issues or situations, (...) for the lessons to be carried out separated by gender." (Federal Ministry for Education, Science and Culture 2011, p. 21f).

Improving motivation

How can gender-sensitive work on and in the school take place, so that motivation and academic performance (in particular) of the boys can be improved? Selected aspects should be identified at four different levels (not exhaustive).

1. Lesson content

> Internal school curricula must be set up and teaching materials should be selected in such way that dealing with gender issues and a gender-sensitive approach are made possible. The teaching and learning materials should deviate from traditional male norms. They should correspond to the interests and different previous experiences of both sexes. In addition, all teaching and learning materials should value the strengths of both sexes, creating another approach towards the so long unfamiliar and new.

2. School (School culture)

> Quality standards for equality must be firmly anchored in the mission statement of the school. Equal rights for girls and boys (and male and female teachers). The school as an institution is responsible for the staff on its payroll. The regular professionalisation of teachers is obvious. The initiative therefore, lies both with the teachers and with the school administration. Professional guidance for girls and boys may decisively contribute to the reduction of traditional role patterns and stereotypes. The selection of appropriate teaching and learning materials as well as intensive work with parents regarding the professional orientation of their children are particularly important here. The implementation of 'girls-days' and 'boy-days' raises awareness of gender issues. The integration of parental involvement in school life – both mothers work and fathers work – can be used by the school body to address gender issues and to bring these into the consciousness of girls and boys. Also working with foreign parents can – in terms of understanding other cultures – occupy an important place. The implementation of gender-related projects (for example 'girls-days') should not be understood

solely as a (stand-alone) event – on the contrary: gender education processes should be and become part of daily school life.

3. Interaction

Female and male teachers must be able to reflect on their own roles – to be a role model, making a decisive contribution to raising awareness of gender issues. Teachers should talk in a gender-neutral language. They should be aware of expectations and stereotypes and be careful not to fall into certain patterns (for example to commend girls for their diligence and boys for their performance). This includes clearly the ability of female and male teachers to perceive girls and boys in their gender-specific embossments. Just as the cooperation with parents make for an important contribution to gender-sensitive behaviour, cooperation with external partners (recreational facilities, etc.) should be taken into account.

4. Organisation (and didactics) of teaching

The promoting of the talented and the social training of disadvantaged girls and boys goes without saying and should therefore not be further analyzed. Initially the existence of profound didactics for gender-equitable education was questioned. If there were these didactics, the question for single-sex and/or coeducational institutions would be less (or not) relevant. But, and this is confirmed by the studies of Woodward, Fergusson, Harwood, i.e., learning situations in single-sex classes result in a higher motivation of boys and girls and to better learning outcomes (compared with coeducational classes). Nevertheless, it should be emphasized that previously redeveloped proposals to improve the teaching methods from a gender perspective are still lacking a systematic analysis and the empirical evidence of efficacy, as stated by Niederdrenk-Felgner, dealing with issues of gender-specific didactics (particularly in mathematics). To speak of separate didactics for boys or for girls, seems inappropriate. Rather, selected didactic and methodological approaches and accesses are necessary to positively influence the motivation of girls and boys and in their consequence lead to better learning outcomes. These include for example:
- Project-oriented teaching and group work: With a comprehensive analysis of a problem, gender-homogeneous groups can come together and generate together ideas for solutions. The social skills of girls would be more recognized and the skills of boys would be much better promoted and strengthened.
- Open learning (individual work): Through internal differentiation measures, the learning is individualized and may lead to the aforementioned results. This may, for example, include a variety of physical activities through which the increased urge to move of the boys is met.
- Forms of conversation in the classroom: To avoid and overcome comprehension problems, in appropriate situations communication should be held (much) more in colloquial speech.
- Open classes – Temporary waiver of coeducation: Even if this requires special skills of the teachers, in a mixed gender class, group work can take place in single-sex groups. The waiver of coeducation in a mixed class can increase the motivation of boys and girls (see also project work).

To make lessons (methodologically) gender-sensitive, means to use forms of open education, through which independent learning becomes possible, for example action-oriented learning, project-based learning, group work, etc. "Because these considerations double immediately the heterogeneity of the student body (...): Students can bring aboard their respective interests much more and establish many social relations. Thus they also learn to recognize their individual personality." (GEW 2007, p. 26)

Methodological issues

The inconclusive results might be driven by methodological issues. In a recent meta-review, Pahlke et al. (2014) show that the methodology matters for the direction and size of the effect. In particular, they observe that studies without a control group show some modest advantages for single-sex education, for both girls and boys. Studies with a proper control group indicate little effect of single-sex education, while experimental studies do not support any benefit from single-sex education.

Looking at earlier literature, we can distinguish six issues which prevent us to draw from earlier literature causal conclusions on the effects of coeducation. A main reason for this lack of causal evidence comes from the longitudinal data where the studies rely on. First, longitudinal data are prone to selection effects. Students (and their parents) who select themselves in single-sex schools have other aspirations and expectations about education and society than students who select themselves in mixed-sex schools. By simply comparing the motivation, classroom climate or educational attainments in both groups, biased evidence will be observed. This is the case in, e.g., Younger and Warrington (2005).

Second, the unit of analysis is often the class or the school. Given the existence of peer-effects, this creates a clustering of standard errors. While classes and schools have numerous pupils, due to the clustered standard errors, the effective unit of observation decreases dramatically such that the internal validity of the results can be questioned. An example of a similar bias can be found in Jackson (2002).

Third, there might be various sources of unobserved heterogeneity influencing the results. Many longitudinal studies lack information on the teachers' perceptions and stereotypes, the pupils' motivation or the parental interest in schooling. Similar unobserved heterogeneity might result in biased estimates. For example, if teachers' stereotypes result in a different attitude towards pupils, the observed differences in (existing) coeducational classes might be overestimated.

Fourth, some studies are prone to a 'Hawthorn effect'. If respondents know that they are subject of a research, they will answer differently – for example, more socially accepted answers. An example of a similar bias can be found in Martino and Meyenn (2002) who made a qualitative research on teachers' perceptions.

Fifth, some studies have only a limited number of observations. This limits the internal validity of the results. For example, the results of Martino and Meyenn (2002) draw on 7 interviews, Martino (2001) is based on a survey of 42 boys, while Sukhnandan et al. (2000) uses 19 case studies.

Using a large experiment with random assignment at the pupil level and with a combined quantitative and qualitative identification strategy, this chapter avoids the previous shortcomings and biases.

3. Flemish education system

The Flemish educational system foresees compulsory education until the age of 18. Its education is structured along nursery (age 2.5 until 6), primary education (6 until 12), secondary education (12 until 18) and higher education (from 18 years onwards). The Flemish school system draws on a few general principles (for an extensive discussion, see www.flanders.be). First, primary and secondary schools are financed by the government and are free of charge for parents. In nursery and primary education, parents are even exempted from paying school materials and school related activities. Second, there is freedom of education such that (1) every person has the right to organize education and establish institutions for this purpose and (2) parents and children have the right to choose a school. Thanks to this freedom of education, a large majority of the students attend publicly subsidized private catholic schools (68%), while only a minority of the students (15%) attend community education. The remaining 16% of the students attend subsidized publicly run education. Third, all children receive equal opportunities in education. Therefore, the government foresees significant resources for student counseling and extra support for additional needs provision.

Secondary education (the education level of interest for this chapter) is structured along three stages of two years. The majority of the teaching periods in the first stage are devoted to the core curriculum (math, languages). From the second stage onwards, there is some form of ability tracking. First, general education (aso) prepares students for higher education. Second, technical education (tso) focusses on technical subjects and prepares its students for a profession or for higher education. Third, secondary arts education combines broad general education with active arts practice. Finally, vocational education (bso) is practice-oriented and prepares students for a specific occupation. A commonly agreed disadvantage of the four forms of secondary education is that general education is higher perceived than the other forms. This creates an unequal composition of the ability groups in that children from higher socio-economic status (SES) groups are overrepresented in general education, while children from lower SES groups are overrepresented in vocational education. This system shortcoming, combined with the high number of early school leavers (i.e., youngsters below the age of 23 who leave education without a higher secondary degree) is the main motivation for a serious reform of the secondary education system by 2016.

Regarding coeducation, since the Second World War, an increasing amount of public schools became coeducational. By the early 1970, also the private Catholic schools followed. By the 1980s, most schools were mixed, although only on January 26, 1994 the law obliged schools to be coeducational. While today schools cannot refuse pupils on the grounds of gender, there is an increasing interest in single-sex education. Some middle schools offer parents the choice for single or mixed-sex education. While there is no empirical evidence, they argue that single-sex education allows teachers better to 'deal with difficult' students (Klasse, 2010).

The only existing study regarding coeducation in Flanders estimates in a longitudinal design the differences in learning outcomes and academic discipline between single and mixed-sex schools (Brutsaert, 2001). He observes that there are no clear advantages (nor disadvantages) of coeducation in Flanders.

While the number of boys equals in secondary education the number of girls, this is not the case for their teachers. About 32% of the teachers in secondary education are male, while 68% are female. This gender imbalance is even larger in primary education where 86% is female. While most of the teachers are female, a large majority of the school management are males.

4. Data and experiment

To examine the impact of coeducation versus single-sex education, we run an experiment in a large Flemish school. The school is located in the area of Brussels (i.e., Herzele). It has both the general education track (aso) as well as technical education (tso). The student population of the school is representative for other Flemish schools – it does not attract a specific socio-economic status group, nor a specific gender or ability group. It has about one third of male teachers, and a female school management.

By running an experiment, the researchers can perfectly control all observed pupil characteristics (e.g., gender, prior class and earlier test scores). As all observed characteristics are randomly distributed across control and treatment groups, we can effectively assume that also unobserved characteristics are randomly distributed across both groups. The experiment is therefore not prone to omitted variable bias as in earlier studies on single-sex education.

The experiment took place on two different days on which we focussed on two different age groups. A first age group are students between 12 and 13 years old, while a second age group are 13 till 14 years old students. We included those two age groups as an a priori power analysis reveals that these include a sufficient number of students to find with a reasonable probability an effect. Before the experiment took place (i.e., during regular education), these students are grouped in 10 mixed classes (5 per age group) of, on average, 20 students. The experiment involved one full day of teaching in the experimental setting.

Random assignment

We randomly assigned students to (1) a boys-only group, (2) a girls-only group, and (3) two mixed-sex groups. A first mixed-sex group had exactly the same amount of girls as boys, while a second mixed group had more boys than girls for the age group 13-14 and more girls than boys for the age group 12-13. The descriptive statistics in Table 1 indicate that besides for gender, the groups were perfectly equal on all observable characteristics, including average school exam scores (only available for age group 13-14). We can therefore assume that also on the unobservable characteristics (e.g., income of the parents, socio-economic status) the groups are equal in expectation.

Timing and tests

The experimental days took place as follows. In the first 15 minutes of the day, all students received some general information about the day. They were told that they would follow 'an international day' in which they receive didactical content which is made by school partners in various European countries (including UK, Turkey, Austria, Norway and

Poland). The students were not informed about the experimental setting, nor about the true purpose of the day. At the end of the 15 minutes, they were regrouped in the new groups according to the random group assignment by the researchers. Next, each group of students went to a particular class where they received during one hour a course about sexuality, interculturality or lifestyle. After a break of 30 minutes, the students went to a different course. The structure of the day is visualized in Figure 3-3.

To avoid biases arising from differences in the teaching style, the same teacher taught the same content (to different groups) the whole day. At the end of each class, students filled out a motivation questionnaire, which is a short version of the 'Motivated Strategies for Learning Questionnaire – MSMQ (the questionnaire is included in the appendix). The scale reliability coefficient (cronbach's alpha) for the questionnaire is 0.86, which indicates a high internal consistency.

Besides these quantitative assessments, there was also an observer in the class who made a qualitative analysis of the differences between the student groups. The qualitative analysis aimed to complement the quantitative findings. Similar to the teacher, the observer followed four times the same subject. The focus of the qualitative assessment lied on the attitude of students and the teacher during the course, the classroom management, the class dynamics and the peer-effects. The observers were experienced teachers with some basic knowledge of qualitative analysis.

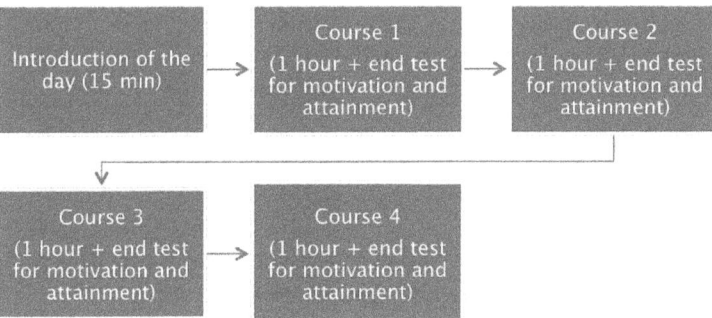

Figure 3-3 Structure of the day – Each course takes one hour, is taught by the same teacher, observed by the same observer and ends with a motivation and educational attainment test

Course content

As the experiment took only one day, we tried to maximize its impact by focusing on 'sensitive' issues as interculturality, sexuality or lifestyle. Thanks to this course content, we can estimate an upper bound impact of single-sex education versus coeducation. For this purpose, we found interesting, publically available, course content on the website of an European project 'Education and Gender'. This content was slightly adapted to the Flemish setting. The full content is available on the following website: http://www.education-and-gender.eu/edge/index.php/en/ects-en.

5. Quantitative analysis

Descriptive statistics

The descriptive statistics are presented in Table 3-1. Group 0 denotes the single-sex group with only boys, group 1 and 2 are the mixed-gender groups, while group 3 is the girls-only group. In group 1 there are more girls for age group 12-13 and more boys for age group 13-14, while group 2 has an about equal percentage of boys and girls. Thanks to the randomization, there are no significant differences between the four groups on the average school grade (only available for age group 13-14). Table 3-1 indicates that students were also effectively reshuffled among the original class groups. Note that information on the educational attainments is only available for some courses, such that this variable has a lower number of observations. The descriptive statistics are roughly the same for the two age groups separately. To save space, they are available upon request.

Group	Variable	n	Mean	S.D.	Min	Max
Boys-only (group 0)						
	Gender (boys = 0)	308	0.00	0.00	0.00	0.00
	Regular class	308	3.25	2.46	0.00	8.00
	Average exam score*	161	70.88	7.91	57.11	88.23
	Post-test: Motivation	308	3.87	3.15	1.22	28.60
	Post-test: Educational attainments**	129	6.53	2.81	0.00	10.00
Coeducation but unequally distributed in gender (group 1)						
	Gender (boys = 0)	327	0.61	0.49	0.00	1.00
	Regular class	327	3.53	2.39	0.00	8.00
	Average exam score	154	69.74	17.28	0.00	83.77
	Post-test: Motivation	327	3.86	2.73	1.40	20.86
	Post-test: Educational attainments**	135	6.82	2.92	0.00	10.00
Coeducation and equally distributed in gender (group 2)						
	Gender (boys = 0)	313	0.53	0.50	0.00	1.00
	Regular class	313	3.78	2.27	0.00	8.00
	Average exam score*	147	71.83	6.26	59.63	86.47
	Post-test: Motivation	281	4.30	4.50	1.40	35.25
	Post-test: Educational attainments**	125	6.34	3.02	0.00	10.00
Girls-only (group 3)						
	Gender (boys = 0)	312	1.00	0.00	1.00	1.00
	Regular class	312	3.76	2.46	0.00	8.00
	Average exam score*	147	73.82	7.82	55.83	85.80
	Post-test: Motivation	312	3.71	2.97	1.43	24.50
	Post-test: Educational attainments**	129	6.78	2.96	0.00	10.00

Note: Except for gender, there are no significant differences in observed characteristics between the four groups. (*) Average school grades are only available for age group 13-14. (**) Educational attainments is only available for some courses, such that this variable has a lower number of observations

Table 3-1 Descriptive statistics

Regression specification

To control for observed heterogeneity in the sample, we estimate the following regression specification:

$$Y_{i,j} = \beta_0 + \beta_1 \text{group}_i + \beta X_i + \varepsilon_i \qquad (1)$$

where $Y_{i,j}$ denotes the post-test on motivation or educational attainments of student i in course j. It should be noted that thanks to the randomization the prior motivation and educational attainments of the students will be equal across all groups, such that even in the absence of a pre-test unbiased inference will be obtained. β_0 is a constant, group indicates whether student i was assigned to a treatment (single-sex education) or control group (coeducation). We will also examine alternative specifications in which group denotes the boys-only group (reference group), a coeducational group with unequal gender distribution (group 1), a coeducational group with equal gender distribution (group 2) or a girls-only group (group 3). X is a vector of observed characteristics of the students and ε_i is an i.i.d. error term with mean 0 and a constant variance. Thanks to the random assignment of the students to the groups, we can interpret the estimated correlation of treatment with Y as a causal effect. The coefficient of the group variable is the variable of interest. In what follows below we only present this estimate, although the full regression results are available upon request.

Various alternative specifications of equation (1) are estimated. A first model specification estimates the effect of participation to the experiment. It does not include any variables to capture the heterogeneity among students. A second model specification adds control variables to Model 1. In particular, we add a course fixed effect to capture the heterogeneity that arises from the subject of the course (e.g., lifestyle, interculturality, sexuality). Model specification 3 further adds postcode fixed effects to capture potential heterogeneity arising from peer effects in the neighbourhood the child is living in. Finally, to account for the fact that some students might know each other from their original (traditional) class, we include class fixed effects. The latter capture the heterogeneity arising from the original peer group.

Effect of coeducation on motivation

We first examine the effects of single-sex education versus coeducation on the motivation of students. By running the four model specifications, which gradually add fixed effects, we can test for the robustness of the results. The outcome variable is the average on the 9 motivation questions. The results in Table 3-2 are presented for the full experimental population, as well as for the two age groups separately. The latter distinction might be interesting to reveal potential differential treatment effects for different age groups.

First consider the estimated effects for all age groups. The negative treatment indicator reveals that students in single-sex groups have a lower motivation compared to students in coeducational groups. This effect is significantly different from 0 at 1% level. The effect size (eta², which is the proportion of the total variance that is attributed to an effect) varies between -0.005 (model 1) and -0.019, which is modest. For the relatively large group of 645 students, the R^2-adjusted reveals that we can explain about 27% of the variation in the motivation of students in the most rich model specification Model 4.

If we split the dummy treatment indicator in the four groups, the results in Table 3-2 show that the negative coefficient is mainly driven by the girls-only group who experienced a significantly lower motivation than the boys-only group, which in turn also have a lower motivation in comparison to the coeducational groups.

Effect of Coeducation on motivation		Model 1	Model 2	Model 3	Model 4
All age groups	**Treatment dummy**				
	Constant	4.390***	4.304***	4.513***	4.724***
	Treatment (ref = mixed-sex groups)	-.171***	-.172***	-.219***	-.188***
	n	645	645	645	645
	R^2-adjusted	0.012	0.033	0.084	0.274
	Treatment groups				
	Constant	4.358***	4.272***	4.460***	4.704***
	Group 1 (mixed; ref = boys)	.152**	.150**	.161**	0.067
	Group 2 (mixed)	-0.112	-0.115	-0.055	-0.123
	Group 3 (girls)	-.279***	-.286***	-.293***	-.370***
	n	645	645	645	645
	R^2-adjusted	0.044	0.066	0.112	0.308
12-13 year old	**Treatment dummy**				
	Constant	4.781***	4.806***	4.817***	4.885***
	Treatment (ref = mixed-sex groups)	-.249***	-.249***	-.322***	-.326***
	n	312	312	312	312
	R^2-adjusted	0.037	0.036	0.112	0.183
	Treatment groups				
	Constant	4.348***	4.372***	4.217***	4.351***
	Group 1 (mixed; ref = boys)	.567***	.567***	.631***	.650***
	Group 2 (mixed)	.271***	.271***	.413***	.474***
	Group 3 (girls)	.339***	.339***	.376***	.390***
	n	312	312	312	312
	R^2-adjusted	0.097	0.096	0.165	0.231
13-14 year old	**Treatment dummy**				
	Constant	4.060***	4.019***	4.713***	4.699***
	Treatment (ref = mixed-sex groups)	-0.086	-0.088	-0.118	-.127*
	n	334	334	324	324
	R^2-adjusted	0.001	0.008	0.075	0.080
	Treatment groups				
	Constant	4.419***	4.373***	4.700***	4.6458***
	Group 1 (mixed; ref = boys)	-.256***	-.255***	-.257***	-.319***
	Group 2 (mixed)	-.480***	-.480***	-.422***	-.439***
	Group 3 (girls)	-.981***	-.986***	-.932***	-.987***
	n	334	334	324	324
	R^2-adjusted	0.276	0.288	0.300	0.317
Fixed effects					
	Subject fixed effect		YES	YES	YES
	Postcode fixed effects			YES	YES
	Class fixed effects				YES

where *, ** and *** denote significance at 1, 5 and 10% respectively; full regression results available upon request; model specifications are robust for including previous grade as a control variable (only available for 13-14 years old)

Table 3.2 Regression outcomes for motivation (outcome variable is the average of the 9 questions)

Slightly different observations are made if we examine the two age groups separately. Significant effects are mainly observed for the 12-13 years old children, while for the 13-14 years old children most model specifications do not indicate a significant influence from coeducation. Interestingly, if the four treatment groups are separately compared to the boys-only groups, all estimated coefficients are significantly different from zero. For the 12-13 years old students, coeducation and girls-only groups experience a significantly higher motivation than the boys-only group, while the 13-14 years old students in coeducation and girls-only groups experience a lower motivation than the boys-only group. This makes clear that the age of children matters for the effect of coeducation. For these two groups, younger students like better coeducation than older students.

Effect of coeducation on educational attainments

We next discuss in Table 3-3 the effect of coeducation on educational attainments. Again, three different samples are examined: all students, age group 12-13 and age group 13-14. First, consider the estimates for the pool of all age groups. In contrast to earlier literature, in all model specifications we do not find any significant effect of coeducation on educational attainments. Even the sign of the estimated coefficient differs in direction between the model specifications. This finding is in line with Spielhofer et al. (2002) and Yates (2003), but contrasts findings by Sukhnandan et al. (2000) and Woodward et al. (1999).

For the youngest age group under study, 12-13 years old, we observe a significant difference between boys-only and girls-only groups. In particular, the girls-only group significantly outperforms the boys-only group. This is in line with a large bulk of research stating that girls acquire higher grades than boys. It is therefore not surprising that girls-only groups perform better than boys-only groups in terms of educational attainments. Nevertheless, it has been argued before that coeducation might be a reason for this underperformance of boys (e.g. by Houtte, 2004 and Warrington and Younger, 2003). The experimental evidence in this chapter indicates that it is not the gender class composition which underlies the difference in performance between boys and girls.

Nevertheless, this finding is not confirmed for the oldest age group. A notable exception is the most rich model specification, which captures fixed effects at subject, postcode and class level. For this model 4, we observe a significant lower level of educational attainments in the girls-only group than the boys-only group. However, this model specification can only explain about 8.7% of the observed variance, such that its outcome should be treated with caution.

Effect of Coeducation on educational attainments		Model 1	Model 2	Model 3	Model 4
All age groups	**Treatment dummy**				
	Constant	6.589***	6.057***	6.962***	7.161***
	Treatment (ref = mixed-sex groups)	0,065	0,074	-0,068	-0,049
	n	518	518	518	518
	R^2-adjusted	-0,001	0,030	0,047	0,053
	Treatment groups				
	Constant	6.534***	6.022***	6.730***	6.999***
	Group 1 (mixed; ref = boys)	0,286	0,262	0,327	0,268
	Group 2 (mixed)	-0,195	-0,203	0,018	0,041
	Group 3 (girls)	0,241	0,224	0,218	0,199
	n	518	518	518	518
	R^2-adjusted	-0,001	0,030	0,046	0,051
12-13 year old	**Treatment dummy**				
	Constant	6.712***	6.889***	7.648***	7.660***
	Treatment (ref = mixed-sex groups)	0,326	0,326	0,085	0,110
	n	246	246	246	246
	R^2-adjusted	0,000	-0,001	0,171	0,167
	Treatment groups				
	Constant	6.411***	6.589***	6.994***	7.115***
	Group 1 (mixed; ref = boys)	0,449	0,449	0,549	0,655
	Group 2 (mixed)	0,121	0,121	0,444	0,615
	Group 3 (girls)	1.193***	1.193***	1.028**	1.203***
	n	246	246	246	246
	R^2-adjusted	0,025	0,023	0,185	0,187
13-14 year old	**Treatment dummy**				
	Constant	6.473***	5.737***	5.997***	6.325***
	Treatment (ref = mixed-sex groups)	-0,151	-0,146	-0,494	-0,427
	n	272	272	260	260
	R^2-adjusted	-0,003	0,092	0,083	0,080
	Treatment groups				
	Constant	6.631***	5.900***	5.557***	5.971***
	Group 1 (mixed; ref = boys)	0,148	0,148	0,365	0,141
	Group 2 (mixed)	-0,455	-0,466	-0,205	-0,359
	Group 3 (girls)	-0,647	-0,647	-0,821	-1.035*
	n	272	272	260	260
	R^2-adjusted	-0,002	0,095	0,087	0,087
Fixed effects					
	Subject fixed effect		YES	YES	YES
	Postcode fixed effects			YES	YES
	Class fixed effects				YES

where *, ** and *** denote significance at 1, 5 and 10% respectively; full regression results available upon request; model specifications are robust for including previous grade as a control variable (only available for 13-14 years old).

Table 3-3 Regression outcomes of the treatment variables on educational attainments (outcome variable is an average test score)

6. Qualitative analysis

To open the black box of the quantitative analysis, the experiment also includes a qualitative analysis. The observations by the four observers in the back of the room provide valuable information on the class dynamics, the behaviour of the two genders and the actions of the teachers.

The observers marked significant differences in behaviour between the four randomly divided groups. While the boys-only group was active and participated well to the class, the girls-only group asked less questions, was more quiet, collaborated less, and was more silent during class. It was observed that the coeducation groups had exactly a mix of those two patterns. In general, the observers noted that the more girls in the class group, the more 'relaxed' the group became. Despite this 'relax attitude', half of the observers noted that the girls-only group was the group which was most intrigued by the course content. In the coeducation groups, it is observed that the boys are more actively seeking the attention of the teacher and the fellow students. For example, the enthusiasm to respond to questions posed by the teacher is higher in groups with boys than groups without or less boys. This finding is in line with Martino and Meyenn (2002). The observations are summarized in Table 3-4.

If the observers were asked to place the different groups on an interval scale, they all agreed on the position of the groups. For both age groups and for the four courses, the observers stated that the boys-only group participated much better to the class than the girls-only group, which posed less questions during the class. There does not seem to be a difference between coeducation groups, but rather between gender groups. At the same time, the girls-only group was much more quiet during class, than the boys-only group. Finally, it was observed that the single-sex groups were more able to discuss sensitive and emotional topics in class than the coeducation groups.

Not only the behaviour of the students differed between the groups, but also the behaviour of the teacher changed. It is observed that the teacher had to make a significantly higher effort to convince the girls groups to participate. On the contrary, in the boys-only group the teacher speaks faster and the course content is more quickly discussed (although by the end of the course, the four groups received exactly the same information). Classroom management in terms of law and order in the class and class participation is the most easy for the teacher in coeducation groups. It should be noted that during regular courses, the teachers are also teaching for coeducation groups, which might bias this observation.

Boys only	Girls only	Equally divided	More boys

Class management

'Under control'	Calm	Very good	Very good
Requires more discipline from the teacher	At the end, the teacher has to ask the students not to talk to each other	During the group work, the pupils collaborate well	Few structure
Throw with pencils			Teacher says two times 'do not talk to each other'

A lot of noise

Attitude of the students during the course			
Very vivid	sweet	Boys give a lot of answers, girls do not participate	Boys and girls give answers
Very enthusiastic	Few answers	Motivated	
Everybody wants to present	Not responding		
Students bully the teacher by using a laser pointer			

Dynamics during the class

Very active, positive	Slow (due to the group, not to the teacher)	Excellent	Excellent (but more noise after 40 minutes)
Very tiring for the teacher			
Are there students hiding or asking a lot of attention?			
Everybody is actively involved in the class	All girls hide	4 boys are very active	Nobody is hiding

Table 3-4 Qualitative analysis by observer

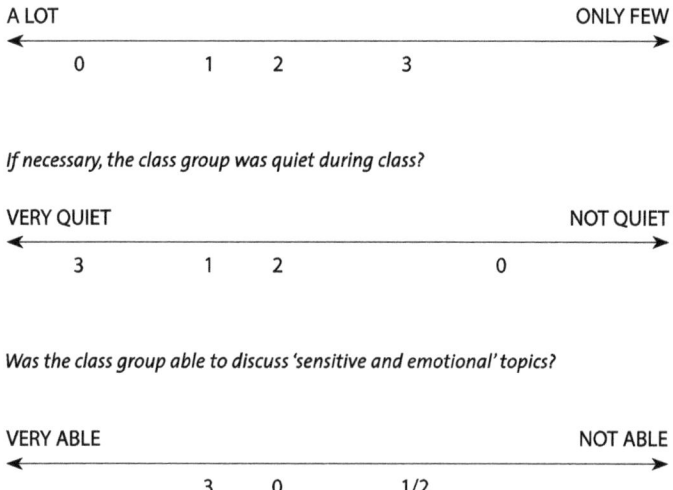

Figure 3-4 Position of the single-sex and coeducation groups on interval scales

7. Conclusion and policy recommendations

Despite being common practice is most western education systems, coeducation is becoming increasingly under pressure. Among other reasons, the lower educational performances of boys have been attributed to the gender composition of classes. In many countries, both progressive and conservative opinion makers argue that single-sex education might be beneficial for both genders. The literature lacks, however, sound empirical evidence which verifies these claims.

This chapter examines by a randomized experiment the effect of single-sex education versus coeducation. By randomizing 12 to 14 years old pupils to single-sex and coeducation groups, we can estimate the causal effect of the gender class composition on students' motivation as well as on educational attainments.

The results reveal that single-sex groups have a significantly lower motivation compared to students in coeducational groups. Analysing the results more in detail shows that boys-only groups outperform the girls groups in terms of motivation. Boys-only groups have a higher motivation than girls and mixed groups. The effect is, however, different for different age groups. For young adolescents of 12-13 years old, coeducation and girls-only groups experience a significantly higher motivation than the boys-only group, while the 13-14 years old pupils in coeducation and girls-only groups experience a lower motivation than the boys-only group. The results of the qualitative analysis confirm that the class dynamics in the single-sex groups are different from the class dynamics in the coeducation groups.

While the effect of single-sex education is rather outspoken for motivation, its impact on educational attainment is modest at best. Only for the youngest age group under study, 12-13 years old, we observe a significant difference between boys-only and girls-only groups. In particular, the girls-only group significantly outperforms the boys-only group. Given the random assignment to coeducational and single-sex groups, the persistent difference in educational outcomes between boys and girls indicates that it is not the gender class composition which creates the different outcomes. Further research should focus on other mechanisms which can explain these differences (e.g., biological differences).

The results provide some interesting insights for policy. First, the debate on the effects of coeducation is too general. Given that its effect on motivation and educational attainments is heterogeneous across different age groups, the debate should be more nuanced and focussed on students' age. Second, as the effect of single-sex education is more outspoken for motivation than for educational attainments, and given that single-sex education is an expensive intervention, policy makers should also explore other tools to foster boys' motivation for schooling.

This chapter provides various lines for further research. First, it would be interesting to add different age cohorts and subjects to the analysis. The differential effects suggest that this might matter for the effects of coeducation. Second, the chapter argued that the experimental evidence provides a higher internal validity than correlational evidence. To increase the external validity of the results, additional experiments should be run, preferable in combination with a mixed-methods set-up. Third, while this experiment provides an upper-bound analysis on the effect, more research is necessary to examine the effects of single-sex education on core subjects as mathematics and languages.

Finally, it should be noted that boys and girls are biologically different. It might therefore not be surprising that the two genders can be motivated by different tools, and that the education system has a different effect on them. The first piece of the puzzle provided in this chapter might indicate a route for further improvement of educational systems, which is not defined on uniform paradigms (e.g., education should be coeducational), but simply on what works best.

References

Alloway, N., & Gilbert, P. (1997). Boys and literacy: Lessons from Australia. *Gender and Education*, 9(1), 49-60.

American Association of University Women (AAUW). (1992). *How schools shortchange girls*. ISBN 1-879922-01-0. Pp. 13.

Brutsaert, H. (2001). *Co-educatie: Studiekansen en kwaliteit van het schoolleven*. Garant.

Cherney, I. D., & Campbell, K. L. (2011). A league of their own: Do single-sex schools increase girls' participation in the physical sciences?. *Sex roles*, 65(9-10), 712-724.

Coffield, F., Moseley, D., Hall, E., & Ecclestone, K. (2004). *Learning styles and pedagogy in post-16 learning: A systematic and critical review*. Learning and Skills Research Centre, London.

Dee, T. S. (2005). A teacher like me: Does race, ethnicity, or gender matter?. *American Economic Review* 92 (2), 158-165.

Finn, J. D. (1980). Sex differences in educational outcomes: A cross-national study. *Sex Roles*, 6(1), 9-26.

Finn, J. D., Dulberg, L., & Reis, J. (1979). Sex differences in educational attainment: A cross-national perspective. *Harvard Educational Review,* 49(4), 477-503.

Guiso, L., Monte, F., Sapienza, P., & Zingales, L. (2008). Culture, gender, and math. *Science* 320(5880), 1164.

Harker, R. (2000). Achievement. Gender and the Single-Sex/Coed Debate. *British Journal of Sociology of Education* 21 (2), pp. 203-218.

Houtte, M. V. (2004). Gender context of the school and study culture, or how the presence of girls affects the achievement of boys. *Educational studies*, 30(4), 409-423.

Jackson, C. (2002). Can single-sex classes in coeducational schools enhance the learning experiences of girls and/or boys? An exploration of pupils' perceptions. *British Educational Research* Journal, 28(1), 37-48.

Jackson, C. K. (2012). Single-sex schools, student achievement, and course selection: Evidence from rule-based student assignments in Trinidad and Tobago. *Journal of Public Economics*, 96(1), 173-187.

Jha, J., & Kelleher, F. (2006). *Boys' Underachievement in Education: An exploration in selected commonwealth countries*. Commonwealth of Learning.

Klasse (2010). Meisjes/jongens. *Education Department of the Flemish Government*. December 24, 2010. Pp. 3.

Lee, V. E., Marks, H. M., & Byrd, T. (1994). Sexism in single-sex and co-educational independent secondary school classrooms. *Sociology of Education* 67, 92-120.

Martino, W. (2001). Boys and reading: Investigating the impact of masculinities on boys' reading preferences and involvement in literacy. *Australian Journal of Language and Literacy*, 24(1), 61.

Martino, W., & Meyenn, B. (2002). 'War, Guns and Cool, Tough Things': Interrogating single-sex classes as a strategy for engaging boys in English. *Cambridge Journal of Education*, 32(3), 303-324.

Munns, G., Arthur, L., Downes, T., Gregson, R., Power, A., Sawyer, W., Singh, M., Thistleton-Martin, J. & Steele, F. (2012). Motivation and Engagement of Boys: Evidence-Based Teaching Practices. Appendices. *Australian Government Department of Education, Science and Training*. Pp. 242.

Nagengast, B., Marsh, H. W., & Hau, K. T. (2013). Effects of single-sex schooling in the final years of high school: A comparison of analysis of covariance and propensity score matching. *Sex roles*, 69(7-8), 404-422.

Ormerod, M. B. (1975). Subject preference and choice in coeducational and single-sex secondary schools. *British Journal of Educational Psychology*, 45(3), 257-267.

Pahlke, E., Hyde, J. S., & Allison, C. M. (2014). The Effects of Single-Sex Compared With Coeducational Schooling on Students' Performance and Attitudes: A Meta-Analysis. *American Psychological Association*. DOI 10.1037/a0035740.

Park, H., Behrman, J. R., & Choi, J. (2013). Causal effects of single-sex schools on college entrance exams and college attendance: Random assignment in Seoul high schools. *Demography*, 50(2), 447-469.

Riordan, C. (1990). *Girls and Boys in School: together or separate?* New York: Teachers College Press.

Rury, J. L. (2008). Coeducation and Same-sex schooling. Enyclopedia of Children and Childhood in History and Society. Accessed by http://www.faqs.org/childhood/Ch-Co/Coeducation-and-Same-Sex-Schooling.html. Date: April 2, 2014.

Sadker, D., & Zittleman, K. R. (2009). *Still failing at fairness: How gender bias cheats girls and boys in school and what we can do about it.* Simon and Schuster.

Shapka, J. D., & Keating, D. P. (2003). Effects of a girls-only curriculum during adolescence: Performance, persistence, and engagement in mathematics and science. *American Educational Research Journal*, 40(4), 929-960.

Spielhofer, T., O'Donnell, L., Benton, T., Schagen, S. & Schagen, I. (2002). *The Impact of School Size and Single-Sex Education on Performance*: National Foundation for Educational Research.

Sukhnandan, L., Lee, B. & Kelleher, S. (2000), *An Investigation Into Gender Differences in Achievement: Phase 2 – School and Classroom Strategies*, London: National Foundation for Educational Research.

Van de gaer, E., Putstjens, H. E., Van Damme, J., De Munter A. (2004). Effects of single-sex versus co-eductional classes and schools on gender difference in progress in language and mathematics achievement. *British journal of sociology of education 3*, 307-322.

Warrington, M., & Younger, M. (2003). 'We decided to give it a twirl': single-sex teaching in English comprehensive schools. *Gender and education*, 15(4), 339-350.

Whitmire, R. (2010). *Why boys fail: Saving our sons from an educational system that's leaving them behind.* AMACOM Div American Mgmt Assn.

Younger, M. & Warrington, M. (2005), *Raising Boys' Achievement*. Report to Department for Education and Skills. Research Report No 636. Pp. 163.

Appendix A

Motivation questionnaire

All questions are on a 6 point Likert scale, where 1 corresponds with 'Totally disagree' and 6 to 'totally agree'.

1. I liked the past course
2. I feel good in this new class group
3. I thought the teacher could handle the class group well.
4. I tried to perform as well during last class because it is important.
5. I tried to perform as well during last class because the teacher expect this from me.
6. I tried to perform as well during last class because I liked the class group.
7. I can work well together with the other students in the class.
8. During last class there were various disagreements (e.g. discussions or quarrels) which disturbed the class.
9. In my opinion, the other students collaborated well during the class.

CHAPTER 4

Benchmarking and Operational Management: an Application of Frontier Analysis to Dutch Secondary Education

Jos L.T. Blank[1]

1. Introduction

Operational management is a topic that is not very popular in many schools. This is not necessarily related to the schools' underestimation of its relevance but could also be because schools prefer to focus on their primary process: offering high quality education. Nevertheless, attention to operational management in education is of eminent importance. Such attention can lead to reduced costs and improved quality, and therefore to a smoother primary process. The lack of indexation of lump sum financing in recent years, an expensive collective labour agreement and planned budget cuts only serve to emphasise the necessity of good operational management.

This chapter offers ways to improve productivity in the secondary education sector by enhancing operational management. The chapter investigates the Dutch education sector as a whole and provides an academic explanation for the chosen methodology. Although the budget shortfall of institutions could also be met by generating extra income (for instance by increasing the financial contribution paid by parents), the income aspect of the budget is beyond the scope of this research.

2. Methodology

In order to answer the research questions empirically, this study uses a cost model. A cost model consists of a so-called cost function and cost share functions. The cost function establishes a link between the cost on one hand and the delivery of services and the prices of the resources used on the other. The cost share functions establish a link between the cost share of a specific resource used, such as teachers, on the one hand and the production and prices of the resources used on the other. From the cost model, various economic relationships derived (see for a discussion Blank et al., 2007; Urlings and Blank, 2012). These include the following relationships:

---

[1] Affiliations:
Delft University, Delft, The Netherlands
Erasmus University, Rotterdam, The Netherlands

- Cost-efficiency;
- Economies of scale;
- Autonomous productivity.

The cost efficiency indicates how an educational institution is performing compared to the best-practice settings, where 100 percent represents a score corresponding to the best-practice setting.

Scale effects are expressed in the cost of flexibility, a number around 1. A value less than 1 indicates that the costs are rising more slowly than production (economies of scale). Scaling leads in that situation to lower average costs. For a value greater than 1 obviously applies exactly the opposite (diseconomies of scale) scaling than cost savings. In practice, we often find that small institutions face economies of scale and large institutions diseconomies of scale.

The autonomous productivity change is derived from the year-on-year changes in costs, after they have been adjusted for changes in production, prices of resources used and operational management of individual institutions. The autonomous productivity change is due to technological, institutional and social changes.

In this analysis, a fairly robust estimation method called the 'thick frontier' is used. In this method, only the best performing institutions (in this case, the best 25%) are used in the estimation of the cost function. Underperforming institutions can cause biases in the estimates. The estimation is conducted in two steps. In the first step the cost function is estimated on all observations. From the estimation results we select the 25% observations with the lowest residuals. The analysis is at school level.

Similar techniques have been used in Bauer et al. (1991), Berger and Humphrey (1991), and Wagenvoort and Schure (2006). In secondary education the methodology is previously tested by Blank et al. (2007).

3. Data

Production

The different types of schools in secondary education require different educational processes and consequently lead to different costs. For example, a teacher who teaches students in the final year of Pre-academic education is generally more expensive than a teacher for students in the first year of vocational training. Therefore, the production cannot be captured in one number. Production indicators are based on the different types of education and grades. We therefore distinct:
- Grade 1 and 2 all types of education;
- Grade 3-6 general education (HAVO - Hoger algemeen voortgezet onderwijs) and pre-university education (VWO - Voorbereidend wetenschappelijk onderwijs);
- Grade 3-4 pre-vocational training (VMBO – Voorbereidend Middelbaar Beroepsonderwijs);
- Remaining education, such as specialized (for pupils with learning disabilities), primary, and senior vocational education.

Quality in education generally is difficult to measure. In order to take the quality of education into account, passes to next grades and examination results are included, where available. The influence of the social background on quality measures are taken into account for by including the accumulated poverty indicator.

The resources

The resources used can be divided into five categories or types of costs:
- Teaching personnel;
- Administrative personnel;
- Executive board and management;
- Housing (excluding rent);
- Material supplies.

We exclude capital cost, because for most institutions local government is responsible for providing school buildings. For a meaningful comparisons with institutions owning their own school buildings rent and amortization of buildings are therefore excluded.

Resource prices

The relative prices of the staff categories are distinct by region and year. Averaging personnel costs per full time equivalent over regions and years by a regression analysis provides a labour price for each staff category for each region in a certain year.

The prices for housing and material are assumed to be equal for all educational institutions and thus only vary over the years. Since housing costs are merely building-related costs such as energy and cleaning energy price indices of the Central Bureau of Statistics (CBS) are used for housing. For the material costs, the consumer price index of the CBS is taken.

Other features

Schools configuration of an educational institution (school size and type of education) partly determines the cost. It is clear that an educational institution with many small schools have a different cost structure than one with a few large schools. To study the influence of the schools configuration on costs, we use the following indicators:
- Average number of pupils per school governed by the educational institution;
- Distribution of students across schools.

The distribution is quantified by means of a so-called Herfindahl index. This index is often used to determine the degree of competition in the market. The Herfindahl index is defined as $I=\sum_{n=1}^{N}S_n^2$ with S_n is the share of pupils in a pre-defined region. A low Herfindahl index indicates many small institutions, a high index of a few dominant large institutions. If there is a strict monopoly the Herfindahl index equals 1.

As characteristics of the business, the following indicators are used:
- average school size;
- concentration of students in a school;
- allocation of resources;
- seniority of staff;
- location size;
- number of branches;
- absenteeism;

- teaching time;
- class size;
- housing;
- ICT.

Data resources, data checks and manipulations

For the analyses we use different databases. The number of pupils is taken from the public files of the Office of Education (DUO), the Ministry of Education, Culture and Science (OCW). The number on education returns are supplied by the Education Inspectorate. The financial data and the data on teaching time come from the database of Windows for Accountability. The staff numbers and salary data are also provided by DUO. Arbo VO has gathered data regarding absenteeism. Finally, the price development of energy and consumer goods and services, as well as the urbanization of the municipalities, are collected by Statistics Netherlands. The period for which all necessary data are available is 2007-2010.

Data checks and manipulations

On these data we applied a number of checks and manipulations (for details see Urlings & Blank, 2012). A statistical description of the data is given in Table 4-1 for the year 2010.

Variable	Obs	Mean	Standard deviation	Minimum	Maximum
Production					
Pupils grade 1+2	271	1,263	2,035	23	24,818
Pupils vocational	271	642	1,088	0	12,558
Pupils general high	271	541	894	0	11,339
Pupils pre-academic	271	600	1,022	0	12,942
Pupils practice	271	58	136	0	938
Pupils primary	271	173	1,155	0	14,977
Pupils senior vocational	271	24	304	0	4,832
Pupils total	271	3,301	5,376	35	62,594
Educational return grade 1+2[a]	271	102	5	85	123
Educational return vocational	271	90	4	73	99
Educational return general high/ pre-academic	271	65	8	41	91
Costs (in duizenden euro's)					
Teaching personnel	271	16,821	27,738	555	317,484
Administrative personnel	271	2,345	4,714	0	56,176
Board/management	271	1,223	2,204	0	21,787
Housing	271	1,601	2,503	6	21,217

Variable	Obs	Mean	Standard deviation	Minimum	Maximum
Material suppliescosts	271	3,789	6,318	94	77,556
Total costs	271	25,778	41,814	734	482,103
Full time equivalents					
Teaching personnel	271	235	384	8	4534
Administrative personnel	271	44	88	0	1004
Board/management	271	12	22	0	228
Prices					
Price Teaching personnel	271	68,874	2,044	65,025	72,708
Price administrative personne	271	50,594	1,584	46,652	52,861
Price board/management[b]	271	105,181	2,769	99,071	109,669
Price housing[c]	271	342	0	342	342
Price material supplies[c]	271	107	0	107	107
Explanatory variables					
Days of absenteeism	177	4.8	2.1	0.0	18.7
Frequency of absenteeism	177	1.4	0.5	0.0	2.5
Schools per institution	271	2.0	2.9	1.0	34.0
Locations per institution	271	4.0	6.5	1.0	71.0
Average school size	271	1,779	1,067	35	8,802
Average location size	271	961	498	35	3,825
Herfindahl-index	271	0.9	0.3	0.0	1.0
Average education time	44	975	38	873	1,058
Share education time> 1,000 uur	44	0.6	0.2	0.0	1.0
Vintage buildings (years)	244	36	18	0	128
ICT-costs total (× 1,000 euro)	39	1,225	1,325	186	5,553
ICT-costs education (× 1,000 euro)	39	887	1,100	88	5,034
ICT-costs operational management (× 1,000 euro)	39	338	471	31	2,832

Table 4-1 Statistical description data, 2010

Secondary education statistics

In 2010, the average secondary school in the Netherlands had 3,300 pupils. Of these, 38% were in the first two grades, 19% in junior vocational education (vmbo), 35% in senior general secondary education (havo) or pre-university education (vwo) and 8% in other education (practical education, primary education or senior vocational education).The costs can be divided across five categories:
- teaching staff (65%);
- administrative staff (9%);
- management (5%);
- accommodation (6%);
- material supplies (15%).

There is a strong variation in the scale of the educational institutions. Half of the educational institutions have fewer than 2,100 pupils and costs of under 17.5 million euros. The largest educational institution has over 62,000 pupils and costs totalling 482 million euros.

4. Results

Reliability of estimates

Urlings and Blank (2012) show that in a statistical sense the cost function model fits the data rather well. Results derived from this cost function are plausible. The cost equation has a high explanatory variance. Majority of the estimated parameters are significant at the 5% level. Most R^2's of the share equations are in line with previous results (Haelermans & Blank, 2012; Haelermans et al., 2012). The requirements on monotonicity and concavity are also fulfilled to a large extent. The monotonicity property tells us that input demand is always positive, which is the case for all observations and in particular for the "average" institution. A necessary condition for concavity is the negativity of the "own" elasticities of substitution. This condition also holds for the "average" institution and is valid for almost all the observations. Finally the condition of negative semi-definite of the matrix of elasticities of substitution holds for the average institution and is also valid in the majority of the observations. We also tested the "significance" of each equation in the system separately by imposing the restriction that all the parameters (except the constant) equals zero. Based on likelihood ratio tests all the null hypotheses were overwhelmingly rejected.

Cost efficiency

Pupil numbers and educational returns (the rate at which pupils progress through the school) on the one hand, and the costs – after correction for price differences – on the other hand, can be used to determine the cost efficiency of each educational institution. Figure 4-1 Distribution of efficiency scores, 2010shows the distribution of the efficiency scores in 2010.

The average cost efficiency equals 91%. This means that by increasing the efficiency, on average 9% of the costs could be saved without reducing the number of pupils or the quality of the education. It is possible that some individual cost efficiency scores may be affected by coincidental or local circumstances that are difficult to influence by management. Therefore, it is important to find out more about the causes of the differences in cost efficiency. Some possible causes are dealt with here.

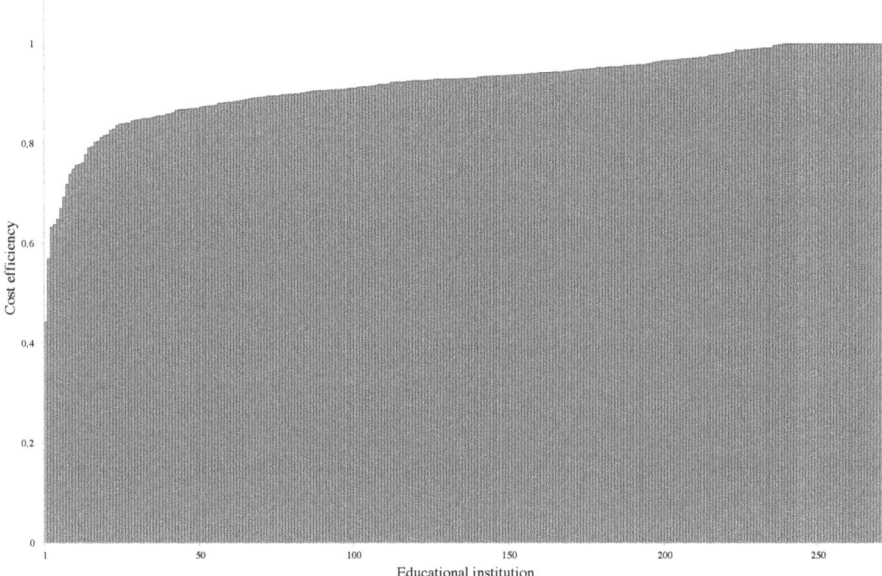

Figure 4-1 Distribution of efficiency scores, 2010

Deciding factors in cost efficiency

Table 4-2 shows the estimated effects of various factors on the cost efficiency of educational institutions. A positive estimate indicates higher cost efficiency and negative estimate lower cost efficiency. The size of the figure is also an indicator of the strength of the effect. In the second column, the unit of measure is shown, for example 1 percentage point, followed by the effect. An increase of absence due to illness by 1 percentage point, for instance, leads on average to a decrease in cost efficiency of 0.9 percentage point. For other units of measure, similar things occur. A growth of 10 percentage point in management experience (length of job duration), for example, leads on average to an improvement in cost efficiency of 1 percentage point.

The effects measured account for almost 39% of the total variation in cost efficiency. In comparison to models estimated for other sectors, this is relatively high.

Property	Unit of measure	Effect (in %-point)[a]
Average school size	1000 pupils	0
Concentration of pupils	0<c<=1	not robust
Over- or underutilisation of management staff	1%-point	-0.9
Over- or underutilisation of administrative staff	1%-point	-0.5
Over- or underutilisation of teaching staff	1%-point	0
Over- or underutilisation of accommodation	1%-point	-0.9
Over- or underutilisation of materials	1%-point	not robust
Experience of management staff	10%	1.0
Experience of administrative staff	10%	0
Experience of teaching staff	10%	-4.0
Average location size	1000 pupils	2.1
Number of locations	1 location	0.3
Average absence	1%-point	-0.9
Percentage meeting the norm of 1000 hours	10%-point	-0.4
Teaching time	hours	not robust
Relative class size	10%-point	3.5
Age of buildings	year	0
Cost share of ICT education	1%-point	0
Cost share of ICT operational management	1%-point	0
Explained proportion of variance	39%	

a 0 = small effect, not significant yet robust regarding different estimations; not robust = strongly fluctuating estimations, high standard deviations in different estimations.

Table 4-2 Effects of properties on cost efficiency

The effects on cost efficiency of the average school size, over or underutilisation concerning teaching staff, experience of administrative staff, age of buildings and the cost shares of ICT in education and operational management, are negligible. It is impossible to determine sound effects for the properties Concentration of pupils, Over or underutilisation of materials, and Teaching time. Those effects appear strongly dependent on the specifications of the model and the selected sample. The remaining effects are significant and robust.

For each educational institution, the optimal allocation of costs among the different categories can be calculated individually. Deviations of the optimum indicate shortage or excess of a certain resource. Each 1 percentage point for shortage or excess leads to a decrease of cost efficiency of respectively 0.9%-point for management, 0.5 percentage point for administration and 0.9%-point for accommodation. If we take into account that for a substantive number of institutions, the shortage or excess is over 5%-point, then the institutions concerned could gain about 2.5%-point in cost efficiency on this aspect. Similar effects are found by Haelermans et al. (2012), Blank et al. (2011) and Blank et al. (2012).

Each 10% addition in management experience (approximated by salary cost per fulltime employee) coincides with a cost efficiency gain of 1 percentage point. This is a striking result. Quality of management can be seen to pay off.

In contrast to the favourable effect of management experience, there is a negative effect for experience (job duration) of teaching staff. An increase in experience (approximated by salary cost per fulltime employee) of 10% leads to a decrease of cost efficiency by 4 percentage point. It should be noted that experienced teaching staff are actually more productive than inexperienced teaching staff. Otherwise, the costs would have grown by 7 to 8% (10% times the cost share of teaching staff).

The scale of the location (accommodation) has a positive effect on cost efficiency. One thousand pupils more per location leads to an increase of cost efficiency of 2.1%. It is clear that scale advantages can be obtained on a location level.

Each additional location has a positive effect of 0.3 percentage point on cost efficiency. This does not mean that distributing the pupils over more locations is favourable (the contrary appears from the scale effect of locations). However, acquiring or starting new locations with new pupils helps to improve cost efficiency for institutions of average size. From this, we can deduce that relatively large educational institutions realise scale advantages with respect to institutions that comprise one school at one location.

Each 1 percentage point decrease of absence due to illness contributes to an improvement of cost efficiency of 0.9%-point. One of the institutions has an absence rate of 18%. This institution therefore has a cost efficiency of only 76%. Reducing absence due to illness to the average rate (5%) would result in a cost efficiency gain of 10.4%-points for this institution.

Institutions are obliged to make sure classes receive a minimum number of hours of teaching per year, depending on the education type and the year. Currently, the norm for most of the educational types and years is 1,000 hours per year. Regarding this norm of 1,000 hours, a 10% increase in the percentage of classes that meet the norm leads to a decrease in cost efficiency of 0.4%. This effect is small but significant. Apparently, meeting the norm leads to additional costs. It should be noted that possible effects on educational performance have been accounted for. A separate analysis of performance on the percentage of classes that meets the norm does not show a significant relationship between both. This holds for all categories of pupils studied.

Class size is modelled by the degree of occupation. This is the relation between the actual group size and a maximum, where the maximum varies according to the mix of the pupil population. For an institution with 1,630 pupils, an average education time 920 hours and 119 fulltime teaching staff (pupil population 43% in the first two years, 34% vmbo and 23% havo or vwo), the group size is 70% of the maximum for such pupil population. An increase in the degree of occupation by 10% leads to an improvement of cost efficiency of 3.5%.

There is an extensive literature on school efficiency (see e.g. Barbetta & Turati, 2003; Millimet & Collier, 2008; Grosskopf et al., 2009; Ni, 2009; Haelermans & Ruggiero, 2013). It is beyond the scope of this chapter to present an overview or comparison of the existing research. For an excellent review of efficiency literature on schools we refer to the thesis of Haelermans (2012).

Scale effects

Scale effects refer to the relation between the size of an institution and the costs per unit of a product or service. Scale advantages arise when the costs per unit decrease when the institutional size increases. Scale disadvantages occur when the costs per unit rise when institutional size increases. Figure 4-2 shows that the graph of the costs per unit has the shape of a hockey stick. The institution size, given by an index, is shown on the horizontal axis. An index of 1 refers to an institution of average size. An index of 2 refers to an institution of twice the size of the average institution. The costs per unit (combination of number of pupils and performance) are shown on the vertical axis. This variable is also given in an index. An index of value 1 gives the costs per unit for the average institution. Small institutions have high costs per unit. These fall rapidly as the size of the institution increases. Institutions of 1 to 1.5 times the average size have the highest scale efficiency. For a larger scale, costs per unit slowly increase once more.

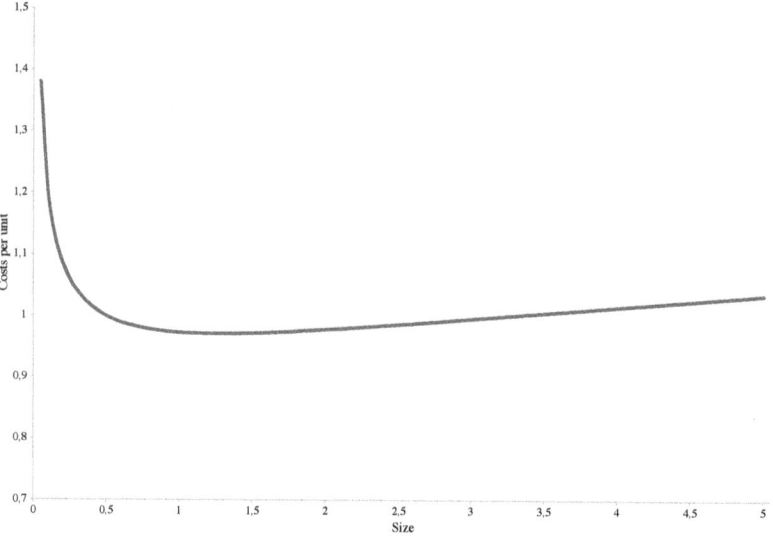

Figure 4-2 Costs per unit as a function of institutional size

Although the optimum size may differ between studies this hockey stick shape is common practice in research. Watt (1980), Bee and Dolton (1985), Smet and Nonneman (1998), and Foreman-Peck and Foreman-Peck (2006) are only a few examples of studies in this area.

Autonomous cost development

The autonomous productivity growth is deduced from the change of costs over time, correcting for changes in production, input prices and operational management of individual institutions. Therefore the autonomous productivity growth corresponds to the productivity growth (lower costs) resulting from technological, institutional or social changes.

The autonomous cost growth with respect to 2007 is shown to be respectively 3.1%, 7.8% and 9.5% for the years 2008, 2009 and 2010. The autonomous cost growth between 2008 and 2009 can be explained by the introduction of "free" study books (almost 5%). Since 2009, schools are obliged to pay for the study books of their pupils. This has led to a significant additional cost that is not related to more production. If we take these extra costs into account then still a serious productivity decline in 2009 and 2010 remains. It is not straightforward where this is coming from, but a study by Haelermans and Blank (2012) may shed some light on this phenomenon. They show in their innovation study that process innovations, teacher professionalization innovations and education chain innovations are positively related to productivity, whereas new courses innovations and pedagogic innovations are negatively related to productivity. It occurs that some of the innovations contribute to extra costs, but not to measurable extra educational outcome.

5. Conclusions

The average cost efficiency of institutions in Dutch secondary education is 91%. This means that educational institutions can reduce their costs on average by 9% without affecting the output of the institution. Although this might give a negative image, it is in line with, or more positive than, studies abroad or in other sectors. Of this 9%, we are able to demonstrate for 3.5% percentage points (39%) how this cost reduction can be achieved. Actual recommendations regarding this are provided in the individual reports that were send to the boards of the institutions, containing specific conclusions and advice for their particular institution.

This study shows that use of resources and absence due to illness are important deciding factors concerning differences in cost efficiency. A small significant effect is found for the percentage of classes that meet the norm of 1,000 teaching hours.

There are also scale effects at the institutional level. Some of the educational institutions are simply too small from a cost efficiency point of view. By mergers and/or increasing pupil numbers, those institutions can still benefit from scale advantages. Conditions for this are the availability of a merger partner in the region, and materialising the scale advantages, for instance by combining staff positions. Scale advantages can only be realised on a limited domain, as from about 1.5 times the average costs, the advantages of scale turn into disadvantages. This means that there are no grounds for advocating unrestrained scale increases. It should be noted that any scale disadvantages that occur are limited. Therefore, the results do not directly indicate that large educational institutions should be split. However, more mergers or takeovers would seem to be undesirable for existing large institutions.

References

Barbetta, G. P., & Turati, G. (2003). Efficiency of junior high schools and the role of proprietary structure. *Annals of Public and Cooperative Economics, 74*(4), 529-551.

Bee, M., & Dolton, P. J. (1985). Costs and economies of scale in UK private schools. *Applied Economics, 17*, 281-290.

Berger, A. N., & Humphrey, D. B. (1991). The Dominance of Inefficiencies over Scale and Product Mix Economies in Banking. [Journal Article]. *Journal of Monetary Economics, 28*(1), 117-148.

Blank, J. L. T., Koot, P. M., & van Hulst, B. L. (2007). Overhead of Onderwijs – Een benchmark van de allocatie van middelen in onderwijsinstellingen voor voortgezet onderwijs. Delft/Rotterdam: IPSE Studies / ECORYS.

Blank, J. L. T., van Hulst, B. L., Koot, P. M., & van der Aa, R. (2012). Benchmarking overhead in education: a theoretical and empirical approach. *Benchmarking: An International Journal, 19*(2), 239-254.

Blank, J. L. T., van Hulst, B. L., & Urlings, T. H. (2011). Does bureaucracy in secondary education increase with time and average school size? A time series and cross sectional analysis. *Bildung und Erziehung, 64*(3), 19.

Foreman-Peck, J., & Foreman-Peck, L. (2006). Should Schools Be Smaller? The Size-Performance Relationship for Welsh Schools. *Economics of Education Review, 25*(2), 157-171.

Grosskopf, S., Hayes, K. J., & Taylor, L. L. (2009). The relative efficiency of charter schools. *Annals of Public and Cooperative Economics, 80*(1), 67-87.

Haelermans, C., & Blank, J. (2012). Is a schools performance related to technical change? a study on the relationship between innovations and secondary school productivity. *Computers & Education, 59*, 884-892.

Haelermans, C. M. G. (2012). *On the productivity and efficiency of education: The role of innovations in Dutch secondary education.* PhD thesis, Maastricht University, Maastricht.

Haelermans, C. M. G., De Witte, K., & Blank, J. L. T. (2012). On the allocation of resources for secondary schools. *Economics of Education Review, 31*, 575-586.

Haelermans, C. M. G., & Ruggiero, J. (2013). Estimating technical and allocative efficiency in the public sector; a nonparametric analysis of Dutch schools. *European Journal of Operational Research, 227*, 174-181.

Millimet, D. L., & Collier, T. (2008). Efficiency in public schools: does competition matter? *Journal of Econometrics, 145*, 134-157.

Ni, Y. (2009). The impact of charter schools on the efficiency of traditional public schools: Evidence from Michigan. *Economics of Education Review, 28*, 571-584.

Smet, M., & Nonneman, W. (1998). Economies of scale and scope in Flemish secondary schools. *Applied Economics, 30*, 1251-1258.

Urlings, T. H., & Blank, J. L. T. (2012). Benchmark bedrijfsvoering voortgezet onderwijs. *IPSE Studies Research Reeks.* Delft: TU Delft, IPSE Studies.

Wagenvoort, R. J. L. M., & Schure, P. H. (2006). A Recursive Thick Frontier Approach to Estimating Production Efficiency*. *Oxford Bulletin of Economics and Statistics, 68*(2), 183-201.

Watt, P. A. (1980). Economies of scale in schools: some evidence from the private sector. *Applied Economics, 12*(2), 235-242.

CHAPTER 5

Schools' Efficiency and Equity: Evidence from a Stochastic Frontier Approach with Translog Specification[1]

Tommaso Agasisti[2]

1. Introduction

The problem of evaluating schools' efficiency is a major economic and policy issue because of the limitations of public budgets. A relevant literature contains many applied studies especially in the US and UK (Johnes, 2004). Usually, efficiency of a school is defined as its ability of transforming inputs (human and financial resources) into outputs (students' achievement); the higher this ability, the higher a school's efficiency score. Therefore, an under-considered issue in the existent literature is the association between their efficiency and equity, the latter defined as the within-school difference in students' achievement. In this chapter, we explicitly consider this indicator among the variables related to efficiency scores; this way the two indicators (efficiency scores and equity measures) can be compared *vis a vis*.

The economic theory suggests that there can be trade-offs between efficiency and equity, to the extent that for improving the former dimension of a school's performance (i.e. the ability of "producing" higher achievement with the minimum level of resources) would require grouping/segregating students by ability or socioeconomic characteristics. However, it can also be the case that the organisation of the educational system, and the instructional process itself, is actually well suited to pursue the two objectives simultaneously. Indeed, the academic literature highlights policies that can foster efficiency and equity at the same time (Woessmann, 2008), and OECD itself confirms, *"The countries and economies participating in PISA demonstrate that excellence and equity are attainable under a wide variety of conditions"* (OECD, 2013; p. 29).

There are two contributions that investigated empirically the associations between indicators of equity and efficiency, at school level – and they have influenced the current

---

[1] We acknowledge the financial support of the Lombardy Regional Government (Project title: "A Report about Lombardy Regional Educational System 2009/10"). We are grateful to the researchers at the Italian National Council for the Evaluation of Schools (INVALSI) for having provided the data and initial statistical assistance. The views expressed in the chapter are our owns, and do not involve the Lombardy Regional Government nor INVALSI. All the eventual errors are our own responsibility.
[2] Politecnico di Milano School of Management (Italy)
Department of Management, Economics and Industrial Engineering
e. tommaso.agasisti@polimi.it

chapter, because their approach is close to the one presented here. Bradley & Taylor (2002) assessed the effect of the pro-competitive policies in England at the end of the 80s, and found that while quasi-markets forces increased (secondary) schools' efficiency, they make the same schools less equal in that social segregation increased. Cherchye *et al.* (2010) propose a nonparametric approach to compare different school types (i.e. public and private) and judge if efficiency scores and rankings are affected by taking equity considerations into account, by measuring the performance of disadvantaged students. The authors, by applying the method to a sample of primary schools in Flanders, conclude that these are relevant for comparing different schools in a 'fairer' way, that is to say considering the multidimensional space of their activities and objectives.

This chapter uses a new dataset of schools located in an Italian Region (Lombardy): it includes 550 primary and 412 middle schools, so that also comparisons of efficiency across different grades are possible. In section §2, we describe the methodology and data, and the section §3 illustrates the results.

2. Methodology and data

The most part of empirical literature that estimated schools' efficiency adopts a non-parametric approach, with particular reference to Data Envelopment Analysis (DEA), while this chapter adopts a Stochastic Frontier Approach (SFA). The former does not require the imposition of a functional form to the production technology (that is difficult to define in education), the latter is superior in considering statistical noise in the empirical analysis, leaving space for inference and robustness checks. An exception is Chakraborty (2009), who explored the efficiency of school districts in Kansas. Moreover, Mizala et al. (2002) and Ruggero & Vitaliano (1999) compared results from DEA and SFA. Excellent reviews of the DEA and SFA literature on education can be found in De Witte and Lopez-Torres (2015), Johnes (2015) and De Witte, Johnes, Johnes, Karagiannis, Portela, Thanassoulis (2015).

This chapter specifies a translog production function, which is flexible in defining the role of inputs in the process; the SFA approach allows including these determinants straightforwardly in the main frontier regression following Battese & Coelli (1995).

In this chapter, the educational production process considers three complementary inputs and two alternative outputs. The analysis is conducted with schools as the unit of analysis. The inputs are:
- *Teach_stud*: teachers_students ratio, capturing human resources' intensity;
- *Expend_stud*: expenditure per student, as a proxy for other financial resources[3];
- *SES*: average students' socioeconomic status, which was included to take into account the background of students' intake.

In the empirical specification, the prices of different inputs were not considered; from a theoretical point of view, it would make sense for teach_stud, but teachers' salaries are strictly regulated by the Ministry of education in Italy, and are uniform across all the country. The outputs are the school's average score in standardized tests administered by the Italian National Council for the Evaluation of Schools (INVALSI) in two subjects (Reading and Math). All the students (except disabled) must take the test. The tests are different in grades 5 and 6, as they measure grade-specific competences and are not built

---
[3] Expend_stud does not include salaries for tenured staff.

for maintaining comparability across time; for this reason, we run the analyses separately for the two grades. The test's score is standardized between [0; 100] – that is, percentage of right answers.

A translog production function was specified, coherently with previous literature in the field (Adkins & Moomaw, 2003); mathematically, the following equation has been estimated:

$$\ln Y_i = \sum_{m=1}^{3} \alpha_m \ln x_{mi} + \frac{1}{2}\sum_{m=1}^{3}\sum_{n=1}^{3} \alpha_{mn} \ln x_{mi} \ln x_{mi} + \varepsilon_i \qquad (1)$$

where there are m inputs (see above) and Y_i is the average achievement score of the ith school. Three models were estimated, for each output, with the aim to test the robustness of results for different specifications: in the Model 1, inputs are Teach_stud and Expend; in the Model 2, Reach_stud and SES; in the Model 3, Teach_stud, SES and Expend. The error term is decomposed to consider the inefficiency term (u_i), as well as factors associated to it (explanatory variables Z_i) and the stochastic error v_i; so that:

$$\varepsilon_i = v_i - u_i \quad u_i \sim N(w_i, \sigma_u^2) \qquad (2)$$
$$w_i = \delta z_i$$

The z-variables are: a dummy for city (against suburbs and rural areas); school's size; variance of socio-economic status (ses_var) and of achievement scores (reading_var; math_var); percentage of female students (%females); percentage of foreign students (%foreign; for middle schools a further distinction is available between %1st_generation_foreign and %2nd_generation_foreign); percentage of disabled students (%disabled); percentage of students who repeated one or more years (%repeating); the share of untenured teachers (%untenured). The choice of limiting the number of inputs, and considering the previous variables as explanatory factors for inefficient schools, is based on a long and solid literature in the field, since Ray (1991) and until recent contributions (Cordero-Ferrera et al., 2008; Chakraborty, 2009).

The error term can be modelled in different ways. In our study, we used two different specifications for each model: half-normal and exponential. As the results are almost identical[4], only those referring to the former are reported.

Descriptive statistics show that the variables generally have similar values for schools in both grades (Table 5-1)[5]; however, achievement scores are higher for primary schools, while resources for middle ones – suggesting a higher technical efficiency of the former.

3. Results and discussion

Appendix A contains the baseline estimations of the production function, for the three different models tested for each output (math and reading); also, correlations among the efficiency scores derived from the different elaborations demonstrates that they

---

[4] Results available on request from the authors.
[5] A wider comment on variables can be found in companion paper (Agasisti et al., 2014), which uses a two-stage DEA approach.

provide very similar results, as relevant correlations are always above 0.93 and statistically significant.

Coefficients for output-to-input elasticity (calculated for the "average" school) reveal that the average students' SES is the factor mostly affecting achievement (Table 5-2). Moreover, while other inputs have different elasticity on math and reading, SES' elasticity is quite constant across grades and subjects – the range is between [0.03; 0.05]. Table 5-3 reports the sample-average efficiency scores for the different models; they are all quite similar, suggesting a good relative efficiency of the educational sector in Lombardy (mean>0.95), and a robustness of results across different specifications. Coherently with expectations from descriptive statistics, primary schools turn out as more efficient than middle schools. Efficiency is strictly related with performance (Figure 5-1), in that there is a clear right-up orientation of efficiency scores with respect to achievement scores, albeit some inefficient schools with high achievement scores, as well as the contrary, do exist.

In the subsequent step, we investigated the factors associated with (in)efficiency. The results of the Battese & Coelli (1995) regression (eq.2) are reported in Table 5-3; they are obtained through Model(s) 3 (for both subjects and grades). Models' diagnostics confirm their stability, as WaldChi2(9) always have p>chi2 that is <.000. Moreover, the values of lnsig2v and sigma_v confirm the presence of statistically significant inefficiency and coherent distribution of the idiosyncratic error. It is important to underline here that the relationships between efficiency scores and covariates must be intended as correlational, not causal (as pointed out by Battese & Coelli, 1995 p. 326: *"(…) Z_{it} is a (1xm) vector of explanatory variables associated with technical inefficiency of production (…)"*). In other terms, the discussion that follows does not individuate if efficiency is determined by a set of factors, or if efficiency is actually causing the correlation with these factors. Albeit the absence of causal design limits the use of the results in a policy perspective; nevertheless, the estimation of the statistical relationship is useful in a descriptive settings – i.e. in exploring which are the characteristics of more efficient schools.

As suggested by the previous literature, the share of foreign students[6] is positively related to inefficiency (performance), as well as the percentage of untenured teachers in primary schools. The main objective of this chapter is to investigate the relationship between efficiency and equity; the latter measured through the variance of achievement scores. Our results suggest that there is not a one-size-fits-all association between efficiency and equity; on the contrary, it seems dependent upon subject and grade. Specifically, efficiency and equity shows complimentary effects in both primary and middle education for Reading; instead, a trade-off seems predominant for Math in middle schools. There are several potential explanations for this finding, and they are beyond the scope of this chapter; therefore, insights from the analyses of cooperative and competitive attitude of students could help in this direction (Bratti *et al.*, 2011).

Nevertheless, the findings have potential policy implications. The most important is that initiatives towards more equity should be grade/subject specific; in some circumstances, there is not statistical evidence of a trade-off between efficiency and equity, although they exist in others. The growing literature about school effectiveness should help in deepening the understanding these types of educational processes' heterogeneity.

---

[6] We have a different indicator for foreign students, as the dataset allowed to distinguish immigrants of first and second generation only for middle schools. The former seem the main cause for lower efficiency, suggesting that probably the same could hold for primary schools.

Primary schools	Mean	Std. Dev.	Min	Max
Reading_score	68.97	3.71	59.02	78.06
Math_score	62.78	4.22	52.36	73.99
SES	0.97	0.32	0.24	2.43
Expend_stud	570.37	354.78	51.52	5198.56
Teach_stud	0.11	0.01	0.07	0.16
%Untenured	0.17	0.08	0.00	0.54
% foreign	0.14	0.08	0.01	0.61
%disabled	0.03	0.01	0.00	0.09
%females	0.48	0.02	0.41	0.56
SES_var	0.87	0.20	0.29	1.25
Math_var	16.56	1.61	11.46	30.39
Reading_var	16.08	2.11	8.89	24.48
City	0.16	0.37	0.00	1.00
Primary schools	Mean	Std. Dev.	Min	Max
Reading_score	62.49	3.08	52.85	70.47
Math_score	53.57	3.52	45.28	60.28
SES	0.92	0.25	0.45	1.60
Expend_stud	847.56	518.68	58.28	4216.40
Teach_stud	0.11	0.02	0.08	0.35
%Untenured	0.25	0.11	0.03	0.67
% 1st_generation_foreign	0.11	0.06	0.00	0.55
% 2nd_generation_foreign	0.03	0.03	0.00	0.16
%disabled	0.04	0.02	0.00	0.14
%females	0.48	0.03	0.35	0.58
SES_var	0.86	0.21	0.27	1.15
Math_var	17.47	1.33	13.71	21.32
Reading_var	14.46	1.57	10.23	20.28
City	0.12	0.33	0.00	1.00

Table 5-1 Descriptive statistics

	Primary schools		Midde Schools	
	Reading	Math	Reading	Math
Teach_stud	-0.0297	0.0286	0.0890	0.0008
Expend	0.0013	0.0096	0.0121	0.0011
SES	0.0344	0.0488	0.0546	0.0549

Notes: Calculations refer to the Models 3 with explanatory variables for (in)efficiency. All the elasticity's coefficients are computed using inputs' average values.

Table 5-2 Output-to-inputs elasticity

Primary schools				
Model	Mean	St.Dev.	Min	Max
Model 1 (math)	0.952	0.021	0.879	0.982
Model 2 (math)	0.956	0.018	0.896	0.986
Model 3 (math)	0.955	0.019	0.891	0.986
Model 1 (reading)	0.951	0.026	0.858	0.987
Model 2 (reading)	0.960	0.019	0.892	0.989
Model 3 (reading)	0.960	0.019	0.891	0.989
Middle schools				
Model	Mean	St.Dev.	Min	Max
Model 1 (math)	0.927	0.045	0.804	0.985
Model 2 (math)	0.934	0.038	0.824	0.986
Model 3 (math)	0.936	0.036	0.829	0.986
Model 1 (reading)	0.949	0.031	0.831	0.990
Model 2 (reading)	0.960	0.021	0.884	0.991
Model 3 (reading)	0.960	0.021	0.881	0.991

Notes: for both primary and middle schools, the (in)efficiency term is specified as with an half-quadratic distribution.

Table 5-3 Sample-average efficiency scores

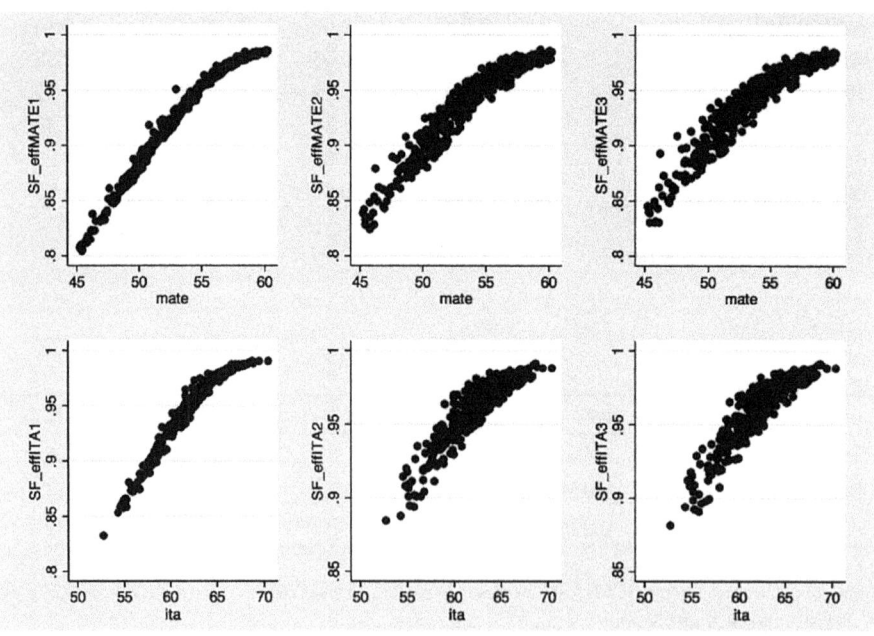

Notes: data sorted on horizontal axis (average school performance).

Figure 5-1 Efficiency scores (y axis) versus achievement scores (x axis)

	Primary schools		Middle schools	
Variables	**Math**	**Reading**	**Math**	**Reading**
City	0.204	-0.447	-0.52	-1.043*
	(0.33)	(0.35)	(0.51)	(0.5)
Size (#students)	(0.002)*	0	0.001	-0.001
	0	0	0	0
SES_var	0.284	-0.025	0.252	0.199
	(0.6)	(0.57)	(0.7)	(0.61)
Math_var	**0.101**		**-0.496****	
	(0.06)		**(0.16)**	
%female (students)	1.328	2.095	-0.769	4.734
	(4.24)	(4.32)	(4.92)	(5.84)
%foreign (students)	3.513*	4.609**		
	(1.62)	(1.75)		
% 1st_generation_foreign			8.654**	9.342**
			(2.86)	(3.05)
% 2nd_generation_foreign			5.917	10.617
			(5.96)	(5.44)
%disabled (students)	2.769	13.279	16.756	18.884*
	(11.08)	(11.09)	(11.12)	(9.46)
%repeating (students)	-9.595	-64.615	10.722	8.43
	(31.3)	(36.98)	(5.64)	(4.64)
%Untenured (teachers)	3.592*	1.511	0.815	0.761
	(1.49)	(1.41)	(1.6)	(1.46)
Reading_var		**0.514*****		**0.318****
		(0.06)		**(0.11)**
_cons	-8.559***	-16.915***	-0.064	-16.290***
	(2.4)	(2.53)	(3.09)	(4.35)
lnsig2v	-5.895	-6.608	-5.952	-6.744
	(.162)	(.119)	(.180)	(.142)
sigma_v	.0524	.0367	.0509	.0343
	(.004)	(.002)	(.004)	(.002)
Log-likelihood	744.470	930.567	581.044	737.161

Dependent variable: each school's inefficiency score (equation [2])

Notes: Standard errors in italics; main variables of interest (equity) in bold.

* Statistical significant at 10%; ** 5%; *** 1%
Reference models: Model 3 – Math and Reading, both grades

Table 5-4 The factors associated to inefficiency. Battese & Coelli (1995) regression

References

Agasisti, T., Bonomi, F., & Sibiano, P. (2014). Measuring the "managerial" efficiency of public schools: a case study in Italy. International Journal of Educational Management, 28(2), 120-140.

Adkins, L.C., Moomaw, R.L., (2003), The impact of local funding on the technical efficiency of Oklahoma schools, Economics Letters, 81, 31-37.

Battese, G.E., Coelli, T.J., (1995), A model for technical inefficiency effects in a stochastic frontier production function for panel data, Empirical Economics, 20, 325-332.

Bradley, S., & Taylor, J. (2002). The Effect of the Quasi-market on the Efficiency-equity Trade-off in the Secondary School Sector. Bulletin of Economic Research, 54(3), 295-314.

Bratti, M., Checchi, D., Filippin, A. (2011), Should you compete or cooperate with your schoolmates?, Education Economics, 19(3), 275–289.

Cordero-Ferrera, J.M., Pedrajia-Chaparro, F., Sainas-Jimenez, J., (2008), Measuring efficiency in education: an analysis of different approaches for incorporating non-discretionary inputs, Applied Economics, 40, 1323-1339.

Chakraborty, K., (2009), Efficiency in public education – the role of socioeconomic variables, Research in Applied Economics, 1(1), 1-18.

Cherchye, L., De Witte, K., Ooghe, E., & Nicaise, I. (2010). Efficiency and equity in private and public education: a nonparametric comparison. European Journal of Operational Research, 202(2), 563-573.

De Witte, K. and Lopez-Torres, L. (2015), Efficiency in Education. A review of literature and a way forward. Center for Economic Studies Working Paper Series. Pp. 42.

De Witte, K., Johnes, J., Johnes, G., Karagiannis, G., Portela, C., Thanassoulis, E. (2015), Applications of Data Envelopment Analysis in Education. In Zhu, J. (Edt). 'Handbook of Data Envelopment Analysis'. Springer Ahead of Print.

Johnes, J., (2004), Efficiency Measurement, in Johnes, G. & Johnes J (eds). The International Handbook on the Economics of Education, 613-741, Edward Elgar Publisher: Cheltenam (UK).

Johnes, J., (2015), OR in Education. European Journal of Operational Research. Ahead of Print.

Mizala, A., Romaguera, P., Farren, D., 2002, The technical efficiency of schools in Chile, Applied Economics, 34, 1533-1552.

OECD. (2013). PISA 2012 Results: excellence through equity – giving every student the chance to succeed (Volume II), OECD Publishing, Paris.

Ruggiero, J., Vitaliano, D.F., 1999, Assessing the efficiency of Public schools using data envelopment analysis and frontier regression, Contemporary Economic Policy, 17(3), 321-331.

Woessmann, L. (2008). Efficiency and equity of European education and training policies. International Tax and Public Finance, 15(2), 199-230.

Appendix A

Results from the (translog) production function (different specifications), and correlations between efficiency scores

Panel A: Primary schools

Variables	Math_1	Math_2	Math_3	Reading_1	Reading_2	Reading_3
teach_stud	-0.939	-1.011*	-0.873	-0.529	-0.566	-0.573
	-0.65	-0.46	-0.63	-0.5	-0.36	-0.49
expend_stud	-0.087		-0.048	-0.038		-0.022
	-0.12		-0.12	-0.1		-0.09
teach_stud^2	-0.495*	-0.452*	-0.428	-0.237	-0.231	-0.236
	-0.23	-0.2	-0.22	-0.18	-0.16	-0.17
expend_stud^2	0.006		0.003	0.004		0.004
	-0.01		-0.01	-0.01		-0.01
teach_stud*expend_stud	-0.024		-0.014	-0.006		-0.001
	-0.04		-0.04	-0.03		-0.03
SES		0.021	0.054		0.099	0.073
		-0.14	-0.18		-0.11	-0.14
SES^2		0.043	0.042		0.001	0.002
		-0.03	-0.03		-0.02	-0.02
teach_stud*SES		-0.017	-0.013		0.022	0.021
		-0.06	-0.06		-0.05	-0.05
expend_stud*SES			-0.004			0.004
			-0.01			-0.01
Constant	3.426***	3.060***	3.348***	3.761***	3.590***	3.629***
	-0.99	-0.51	-0.97	-0.78	-0.4	-0.76
lnsig2v coefficient	-5.788***	-5.821***	-5.844***	-6.569***	-6.419***	-6.426***
	-0.21	-0.21	-0.21	-0.2	-0.19	-0.19
lnsig2u coefficient	-5.535***	-5.726***	-5.675***	-5.496***	-5.929***	-5.926***
	-0.47	-0.53	-0.5	-0.22	-0.34	-0.34

Notes: all the variables are expressed in logarithms

Correlations	Math_1	Math_2	Math_3
Math_1	1.000		
Math_2	0.965	1.000	
Math_3	0.965	0.999	1.000

	Reading_1	Reading_2	Reading_3
Reading_1	1.000		
Reading_2	0.954	1.000	
Reading_3	0.953	0.999	1.000

Panel B: Middle schools

Variables	Math_1	Math_2	Math_3	Reading_1	Reading_2	Reading_3
teach_stud	0.185	-0.164	0.35	0.178	0.042	0.355
	-0.39	-0.2	-0.39	-0.28	-0.14	-0.28
expend_stud	-0.016		-0.096	0.078		-0.008
	-0.11		-0.12	-0.08		-0.08
teach_stud^2	0.021	-0.036	0.012	0.048	0.012	0.044
	-0.05	-0.05	-0.05	-0.04	-0.03	-0.04
expend_stud^2	-0.002		-0.001	-0.006		-0.004
	-0.01		-0.01	0		0
teach_stud* expend_stud	-0.018		-0.046	0		-0.027
	-0.03		-0.03	-0.02		-0.02
SES		0.186	0.134		0.031	0.067
		-0.16	-0.23		-0.12	-0.17
SES^2		0.025	0.033		-0.009	-0.01
		-0.03	-0.04		-0.03	-0.03
teach_stud*SES		0.055	0.047		-0.016	-0.02
		-0.07	-0.07		-0.05	-0.05
expend_stud*SES			0.006			-0.006
			-0.02			-0.01
Constant	4.299***	3.866***	4.752***	4.095***	4.217***	4.585***
	-0.73	-0.21	-0.75	-0.53	-0.14	-0.53
lnsig2v						
coefficient	-6.774***	-6.553***	-6.468***	-7.134***	-6.833***	-6.879***
	-0.42	-0.38	-0.35	-0.24	-0.24	-0.25
lnsig2u						
coefficient	-4.684***	-4.901***	-4.974***	-5.407***	-5.946***	-5.930***
	-0.21	-0.26	-0.27	-0.16	-0.31	-0.3

All the variables are expressed in logarithms

Correlations	Math_1	Math_2	Math_3
Math_1	1.000		
Math_2	0.976	1.000	
Math_3	0.971	0.997	1.000
	Reading_1	Reading_2	Reading_3
Reading_1	1.000		
Reading_2	0.933	1.000	
Reading_3	0.933	0.991	1.000

CHAPTER 6

Do Nurses React to Inter-Industry Wage Differentials? – Evidence of Nursing Graduates in the Netherlands[1]

Sofie J. Cabus[2]

1. Introduction

Education economics is also concerned about the relationship between education and the labour market. The European Center for the Development of Vocational Training (Cedefop) indicates in this respect that `skill shortages', defined as individuals without credentials or skills considered `valid' to enter the job, are underlying recruitment bottlenecks. Recruitment bottlenecks in the life sciences and health industry (LSH) are worrisome, and will become problematic, as in most developed countries, population ageing increasingly put stress on the demand for health care services (Hurd, 1973; Jones and Gates, 2004; Heitmueller and Inglis, 2007; Cedefop, 2010; Maestad et al., 2010; World Health Organization, 2011). There are two broad explanations why skill shortages arise. First, there are not enough individuals who study in the field of nursing, so that, at least in the Netherlands, the demand for nurses is greater than the supply of nurses (Statistics Netherlands). The LSH industry may well suffer from bad image problems, relative to other industries, so that the industry is not able to attract individuals in health and welfare education or training. Second, those who studied in the field of nursing, leave the LSH industry early and, thus, switch to another industry. This chapter particularly focusses on the latter reason of skill shortages in LSH by exploring the labor market prospects of graduates in the field of nursing or midwifery.[3]

The previous literature present several potential reasons of leaving the LSH industry: nurses are underpaid (Taylor, 2007; Di Tommaso et al., 2009); compared to other industries, health professionals and associates have to work hard and irregular hours, and face, in some cases, life threatening risks on the job (Shields and Ward, 2001; Shields, 2004; Yildirim and Aycan, 2008; Di Tommaso et al., 2009); professions as nursing are considered female professions and, thus, less attractive to men (Maestad et al., 2010); the costs (or

---

[1] The paper benefitted from comments and discussions with Wim Groot, Henriette Maassen van den Brink, Kristof De Witte, TIER seminar participants, and participants of the 2014 annual conference of the Society of Labor Economics.
[2] The corresponding author is affiliated with Maastricht University, Top institute for Evidence Based Education Research, Kapoenstraat 2, 6200 MD Maastricht, the Netherlands. Email: s.cabus@maastrichtuniversity.nl.
[3] Throughout this paper, graduates in the field of nursing or midwifery are abbreviated by `nursing' or `nurses'.

student investment) of attending nursing education and training and the lack of student loans (Yett, 1966); and some researchers discuss the work-family conflict (Yildirim and Aycan, 2008). This chapter contributes to the previous literature by exploring the extent to which inter-industry wage differentials can explain the decision to quit LSH. As wages are a composite measure of the return to (innate) ability, education in school, experiences on-the-job, and background characteristics (e.g. Mincer, 1958; Becker, 1962, 1964), inter-industry wage differentials can tell us something more about the demand and supply of nurses' skills, and the return to these skills, in and out of LSH. From this, the rise (and fall) of recruitment bottlenecks, or else the rise (and fall) of skill shortages as a result of switching from LSH to other industries, can be explored. The previous literature on wage differentials focused on differences in earnings by gender (e.g. Groshen, 1991; Jones and Gates, 2004); by race or ethnicity (e.g. Lam and Liu, 2002; Heywood and Halloran, 2004; Heywood and Parent, 2012); by health status (e.g. Johnson and Lambrinos, 1985; and Kidd et al., 2000); or by type of education program (e.g. Booton and Lane, 1985; Gill and Leigh, 2003). This chapter focuses on inter-industry wage differentials for apparently similar workers. The central question of this chapter is then: can an individual, with nursing credentials, who is not employed in the LSH industry but in 'foreign' industries[4], do better than a nurse in LSH employment?

This chapter contributes to the previous literature on inter-industry wage differentials of nursing graduates by the integration of the skill-weights approach (Lazaer, 2009) with an empirical analysis in one country (the Netherlands). To our best knowledge, the fairly recent theoretical model has not yet been applied in previous research, in particularly not in research with regard to employment in the LSH industry. We use repeated cross-section data on the school-to-work decision of about 5,000 nurses or midwives working in the Netherlands in different sectors over the period 2003 to 2011. These health professionals filled in the Dutch higher vocational education school-leaving questionnaires (HBO monitor) one year after graduation from their studies. The fact that nurses are observed very early in their career is considered as a particular contribution of this chapter to the literature, whereas previous work focused on later stages of the nursing career (e.g. Shields and Ward, 2001).

2. Wage differentials and job-related skills in the literature

Old and recent theoretical and empirical studies are discussing why differences in wages between similar workers in different industries exist. We start with the early work of Krueger and Summer (1986). Their work is mainly on the inter-industry wage structure. They argue that across countries: *"[...] the wage structure is very similar for different types of workers. Certain industries pay all types of workers high wages and others paying all types of workers relatively low wages (p.2)."* Krueger and Summer (1986) conclude that the competitive labor market model, in which firms compete against each other, (and which

---

[4] Throughout this paper, we will often refer to the concept of 'foreign industries'. Unless otherwise stated, foreign does not refer to industries in other countries than the Netherlands, i.e. abroad, but other-than-LSH industries. This facilitates the notation.

should impose competitive wages,) should be modified in order to explain the observed inter-industry wage variations. They argue for a non-competitive explanation dealing with efficiency wages and rent-sharing between firms and workers.

Dickens and Katz (1987) confirm these findings of Krueger and Summer (1986). They have analyzed the differences in wages for both union and nonunion workers across time, countries and industries. The authors argue the persistency of these wage differentials, even after controlling for individual background characteristics and job location. Dickens and Katz (1987) also show that individuals who switch from low to high paying industries receive a considerable share of the industry wage premium. They conclude that job-related ability and work experience may play an important role in explaining the persistency of the observed differences in wages, aside from differences in job quality or compensating wage differentials.

Gibbons and Katz (1992) present in their work two different explanations with respect to wage differentials between industries. On the one hand, they argue that the underlying worker population between distinct industries may substantially differ with respect to unobserved job-related ability, so that differences in worker productivity drive the observed wage differential, and not the type of industry (see also Roy, 1951). On the other hand, Gibbons and Katz (1992) argue that, if it is possible to construct a research design wherein apparently similar workers can be compared, then 'true' wage differentials can be observed, in essence, as a result of: (1) compensating wage differentials; (2) rent-sharing; and (3) efficiency wages. Note that these two explanations are also similar to those put forth by Krueger and Summer (1986).[5]

A more recent study of Handy and Katz (1998) provides an example with respect to inter-industry wage structure differences. The authors examine the differences in wages between nonprofit organizations and corporations. Overall, the authors observe lower wages in the nonprofit sector than in the for-profit sector. Handy and Katz (1998) argue that the observed wage differentials are actually advantageous for the nonprofit sector, as it generates consumer trust and self-selection of employees in managerial positions. This selectivity is called positive, as it attracts desirable workers in nonprofits compared to for-profits. Melly (2005) also describes wage differentials between public and private sector employees in Germany. She explores these wage differentials by gender and by educational attainment. The author argues that women have higher differences in wages between the public sector and the private sector than men. Melly (2005) also observes that, compared to the private sector, wages in the public sector are more equally distributed across different educational levels.

Recent previous research also distinguishes between general and job-specific skills. The focus of this evidence is rather on wage growth and earnings profiles than on estimating inter-industry wage differentials. For example, Dustmann and Pereira (2008) analyze the returns to tenure and experience in two countries, namely: the United Kingdom and Germany. Taking two countries, the authors aim at exploring how wages are affected by two totally different labor market regulations and training systems. They find that a flexible labor market system, such as in the UK, yield higher returns to experience,

---

[5] Having both explanations empirically tested, Gibbons and Katz (1992) conclude that there is no theoretical model in the literature that is able to motivate their estimated wage differentials between industries.

than the German system with relatively strict employment protection. Dustmann and Pereira (2008) argue that, owing to the German apprenticeship system, graduates from vocational education have higher wages in the short run. However, in the long run, wage growth of these graduates is limited, flattening life-time returns to experiences. These short run and long run labor market outcomes are also observed by Hanushek et al. (2011) for 18 countries, and Cabus and Haelermans (2013) for the Netherlands.

Relatively new in explaining inter-industry wage differentials, is the skill-weights approach of Lazaer (2009). The author modeled a skill-weights approach particularly for understanding wage differences between stayers (those who stay in the industry) and leavers (those who switch industry).[6] The starting point is that credentials signal two types of skills: (1) general skills; and (2) industry-specific skills. For instance, the former type of skills can be used in the LSH and the foreign industry, whereas the latter only contribute to the productivity at the LSH industry. Lazaer (2009, p.914) argues in this respect: *"Firm-specific human capital raises the productivity of the worker at the current firm, but not elsewhere, setting up a bilateral monopoly situation between the worker and firm."* The skills-weights approach puts forth that not all industries attach the same weight to the skills an individual acquired in his/her (school) career. For instance, the LSH industry attaches high weights to health and welfare skills, such as taking blood from a patient. These skills are considered irrelevant in foreign industries (e.g. a nurse who would become a saleswoman in a department store). In conclusion, the skill-weights model predicts that nurses switch to foreign industries in case their general skills pay-off more in foreign industries than seniority in LSH. It also predicts that industries in need of rigorous specific (vocational) skills are prone to recruitment bottlenecks.

3. The life sciences and health industry in the Netherlands

Facts and figures

This chapter explores the employment decision of graduates in the field of nursing in the Netherlands. The LSH industry in the Netherlands is an interesting case study for at least three reasons. First, the life sciences and health industry is a top industry: it captures about 14.9 percent of the Dutch Gross Domestic Product (i.e. an investment per capita of about €5,392); the industry is considered an important employer giving work to 178,435 nurses and 43,630 life sciences and health professionals (Statistics Netherlands, 2012); and the total revenue of the life sciences and health industry is estimated at 17.7 billion euros in 2010 (Dutch life sciences outlook, 2012; Statistics Netherlands, 2011).

Second, there is a lively policy debate in the Netherlands on health professionals' labor market prospects in the LSH industry. The Amsterdam Economic Board argues in their `Human Capital Agendas' that managing talent will play a critical role in innovation and growth of the LSH industry (see Amsterdam Economic Board, 2012). In this respect, the LSH industry formulates three goals: (1) to develop new or change old education or training programs in accordance with the development of the LSH industry; (2) to

---

[6] Note that we adapt his general theory directly to the choice of working in the LSH industry. Thus, Lazaer (2009) did not use nursery as an example in his work.

foster close cooperation between modern LSH activities, the companies in the industry (regional or national), and LSH education or training programs; and (3) to improve job attractiveness of the LSH industry.

Third, government officials recently discussed policy measures in order to cut health care costs in 2014 (rijksoverheid.nl, 2013). If government officials and policy makers would make the LSH industry less attractive, relative to other industries, then this calls for an in-depth research on the consequences for (the attractiveness of) employment in the LSH industry.

Wage setting of nurses

In the Netherlands, nurses earn an average gross monthly wage of 2,725 euros when working 40 hours per week and 4.33 weeks per month. Comparing the Dutch gross monthly wages to those of the neighboring countries, 3,833 euros in the United Kingdom, 3,241 euros in Belgium, and 2,858 euros in Germany, it is concluded that nurses' purchasing power parities in the Netherlands are ranked latest (Kevätsalo, 2007; loonwijzer.nl, 2014). Note that, in the Netherlands, the majority of nurses working in the LSH industry are having a part-time contract. This is not surprisingly, given that the union density is relatively low in the Netherlands (i.e. the lowest compared to UK, Belgium, and Germany), and given that LSH employers are often third sector organizations.

4. Conceptual framework

In the first instance, the theoretical model used in this chapter aims at offering an interpretation of wage differentials between LSH and other, 'foreign' industries, by using the skill-weights approach of Lazaer (2009). Note that 'foreign' in this context does not refer to industries in other countries than the Netherlands, i.e. abroad, but other-than-LSH industries. It facilitates the notation as follows. In the second instance, the theoretical model offers an interpretation for skills shortages in LSH, as a result of switching to other, 'foreign' industries by using the concept of *market thickness*.

Inter-industry wage differentials

The starting point is that every nurse has two types of skills A and B. Let A denote the general skills, and B the industry-specific skills, so that every nurse has a skill set (A, B). The weights attached to the skill set of the nurse in the LSH industry is denoted by λ_1, whereas the weights attached to skills in the 'foreign' (F) industry is denoted by λ_2. Note that $\lambda \sim U[0,1]$ follows a uniform distribution. Following Lazaer (2009), we present the output of a nurse in the LSH industry as $\lambda_1 A + (1-\lambda_1)B$, and the output of a nurse in the F industry as $\lambda_2 A + (1-\lambda_2)B$. Nurses are paid according to their output in each industry.

There are two periods $t \in \{1,2\}$. In the first period (t=1), the individual graduates from health and welfare education or training. In the second period (t=2), a nurse can make a decision between staying in the LSH industry or leaving to the F industry. The level of the wage (W) a nurse will earn in the second period is equal to the return to the skill set (A, B). If a nurse decides to stay in LSH, the outside offer λ_2 will be rewarded as `seniority'. In order to stay in LSH, the outside offer λ_2 should be worse than the LSH job offer λ_1. Otherwise, the nurse could do better elsewhere, so that she decides to leave LSH voluntary. As such, the main assumption underlying the skill-weights approach is that nurses only quit in case they would do better elsewhere. The wage of an individual who stays and who leaves can then be formally expressed as (Lazaer, 2009, p.920):

$$W_{stay} = B + \tfrac{1}{2}(\lambda_1 + E(\lambda_2|\lambda_2 < \lambda_1)(A-B) , \qquad (1)$$

$$W_{quit} = B + \tfrac{1}{2}(\lambda_1 + E(\lambda_2|\lambda_2 > \lambda_1)(A-B). \qquad (2)$$

Consequently, the inter-industry wage differential between nurses who quit and who stay can then be formally expressed as (Lazaer, 2009, p.924):

$$W_{quit} - W_{stay} = \tfrac{1}{2}[E(\lambda_2|\lambda_2 > \lambda_1) - E(\lambda_2|\lambda_2 < \lambda_1)](A-B) ,$$

$$W_{quit} - W_{stay} > 0 , \qquad (3)$$

where the expression (A−B) denotes the difference between general skills and industry-specific skills, and the estimated wage differential is unambiguously positive. Note that specific skills B are cancelled out from equation (3) when subtracting W_{stay} from W_{quit}.

Market thickness

Market thickness particularly deals with (A-B). Consider the following two extreme cases: (1) very thick markets; and (2) very thin markets. In the extreme case that there would only be one industry, the LSH industry, and no other industries, having nursing credentials would become obvious for an individual to connect with the labor market, so that these skills are considered general. Consequently, if the LSH industry is thick, then nurses get more offers from which they can choose. In this extreme case, (A−B) is equal to zero and one would not estimate a wage differential ($W_{quit} - W_{stay} = 0$). However, in the extreme case that the market is very thin, industry-specific skills are not transferable to other, foreign industries. If there would be only one industry, the LSH industry, wherein nursing credentials are suitable, among many other foreign industries, health and welfare education or training becomes a risky investment because: *"[...] wage loss associated with job turnover is greater in very thin markets than in very thick markets (Lazaer (2009, p.925)."* Thus, the average wage offer (λ) on the foreign labor market for an individual who heavily invested in B, and not in A, will be worse compared to individuals who heavily invested in A, and not in B. Thus, the thinner the market, the higher the risk of investment in B in terms of bad labor market outcomes. Thin markets are, therefore, prone to recruitment bottlenecks.

5. Empirical strategy

The intuition

Estimating inter-industry wage differentials induce problems of self-selection of individuals into LSH employment (Rubin, 1974). For instance, women are more likely than men to become nurse or midwife (Jones and Gates, 2004). Individuals may have an entirely different motivation to work in LSH, simply based on gender, race or ethnicity, or cultural differences. However, we argue that these determinants of motivation also play a key role in enrolling in health and welfare education or training necessary to perform in an LSH job. The probability that an individual will start in an LSH profession depends on studying in the field of health and welfare, and these individual probabilities to enroll in health and welfare education or training reflect the (initial) motivation of students to go into LSH (see also Botelho et al., 1998). Thus, comparing only individuals with credentials in nursing, already enhances comparability between these health professionals in different industries (this is also confirmed in Section 6).

Nonetheless, selectivity bias can still occur at the start of employment: individuals can diverge from their initial thought of going into LSH and, consequently, apply for work in foreign sectors. This decision to 'switch' may be associated with, for instance, individual background characteristics (e.g. gender, ethnicity, innate ability, and motivation), on the one hand, or regional variation in employment opportunities (i.e. the number of vacancies, the availability of hospitals, and structure of the LSH industry) (e.g. Booton and Lane, 1985; Elliot et al., 2007), on the other hand. We deal with the former type of selectivity by using iterative one-to-one matching models. Here, the idea is that individuals with nursing credentials who do not work in the LSH industry are matched, based on their general job-related skills, with individuals having the same credentials, but who do work in the LSH industry (see also Gibbons and Katz, 1992). Indeed, the mathematical theory (Section 4) shows that, when computing inter-industry wage differentials, nurses' industry-specific skills are cancelled out, and, consequently, do not give rise to the estimated inter-industry wage differentials. As such, we do not have to match nurses based on job-specific skills. In addition, we only look at nurses who graduated at most one year ago from their studies. Job market experience in LSH is, thus, limited.

General skills will be expressed as an index (see Section 6). They are a composite measure of innate ability, individual characteristics, education in school, and, to some extent, experience on-the-job. Thus, because of matching on job-related abilities, we can control for observed and unobserved differences between nurses' general skills underlying potential wage differences (see critiques of Gibbons and Katz, 1992).

We deal with the latter type of selectivity by using regional fixed effects models. These fixed effects models are particularly useful within the scope of regional variation in employment opportunities, which are considered difficult to change in the short run (e.g. the availability of hospitals).

Formal expression

Consider an individual $i \in \{1,2,...N\}$ who studied in the field of nursing. Having studied in this field is a necessary condition in order to work as nurse, midwife or related health (associate) profession. At time (t=1), the graduated individual has to make a decision to stay in LSH, or to switch industry. Assume that the decision of the individual is based on the attractiveness of LSH at time t, relative to other sectors. We express the level of attractiveness by the hourly wages (y_i) one can earn when working in a particular industry.

Let I denote a treatment indicator that takes the value of 0 if individuals choose to stay in LSH; and 1 if otherwise. We then may write the average treatment effect of the treated as (see Cameron and Trivedi (2005):

$$E(y1_i|I = 1) - E(y0_i|I=0),$$

if studied health profession $=1$, (4)

where $y1i$ denotes the wages observed for a treated student, and $y0i$ the wages observed for a control student.
We can rewrite equation (4) as:

$$E(y_{1i} - y_{0i}|I = 1) + \{E(y_{0i}|I=1) - E(y_{0i}|I=0)\},$$

if studied health profession $=1$. (5)

The first term denotes the average treatment effect of the treated, and the second term the bias that may be estimated owing to self-selection of graduates into LSH employment. Self-selection gives rise to omitted variables bias, in case selection on observable and unobservable variables takes place. In order to deal with selection into LSH employment, we consider the functional form of the labor market outcome 'wages' (Mincer, 1958; Becker, 1962, 1964):

$$y_i \sim f(\alpha_i; v_i; \xi_i; X_{ji}). \tag{6}$$

Equation (6) argues that the level of the wages one can earn in the labor market depends on: (innate) ability α_i; education v_i; experience ξ_i; and a vector X_{ji} of individual, family and neighborhood characteristics. From this functional form of y_i we can argue that untreated students are comparable to treated students, when they have, on average, the same level of innate ability, education and experience. And also based on their background characteristics, they are, on average, the same. As such, if treated and untreated students are comparable as previously argued, wage differentials can only be explained by the hourly wages y_i one can earn when working in different occupations (i.e. LSH, or not).[7] Wage differentials can, thus, be defined as the difference in wages of comparable, homogenous individuals (with respect to $\alpha_i; v_i; \xi_i; X_{ji}$) working in different industries.

An important step in our empirical strategy is to make treated and untreated graduates, on average, comparable with respect to: $\alpha_i; v_i; \xi_i; X_{ji}$ (see also the critiques of Gibbons and Katz, 1992). Therefore, we propose to match individuals, who studied in the field of nursing, and who are not in LSH, to individuals, who also studied in this field, but who do work in LSH. We use iterative one-to-one matching of treated individuals (i.e. those who switch) to untreated individuals (i.e. those who stay) based on their observed set of general skills. We perform 500 one-to-one matching iterations in total, each time using a random sorting of the data. See Section 6 for more information on the validity and reliability of the set of abilities used in this chapter. These abilities are partly endowed (α_i), and have been formed by the family and the neighborhood wherein individuals grow up (X_{ji}), but also by education in schools (v_i), and also by experience on the job (e.g. internships) (ξ_i). Thus, we argue that, under the assumption that the set of abilities measured is sufficiently informative with respect to the individuals (cap)abilities

---

[7] Note that, if treated and untreated students are, on average, comparable, their reservation wage should also be, on average, comparable. In this case, the problem of censored observations is ignorable (see Cabus and Haelermans, 2013).

to perform well in the job, we are able to capture observed and unobserved differences between control group and treatment group with respect to: $\alpha_i; \nu_i; \xi_i; X_{ji}$. Owing to one-to-one matching based on job-related abilities, the distribution of job-related abilities is, on average, the same for treated and matched untreated students. Note that we can test for this latter assumption to hold (see Section 8).

We also condition on the variation in attractiveness of industries between municipalities (m_k, with $k \in \{1,2,...,K\}$). Employment rates can differ between cities in the Netherlands, among other reasons, because of the availability of hospitals, clinics, pharmacy, and other LSH business-related activities. Regional variation can bias the results, as students who have keen interest in studying in the field of nursing, and, consequently, in being employed in a good hospital or care center, are likely to, for example, perform their internship in this good hospital in order to increase their chances on the LSH job market. The attractiveness of LSH employment can substantially differ between municipalities, among other reasons, because of the availability of hospitals, clinics, pharmacy and other LSH related businesses. We deal with regional variation in employment opportunities by using regional fixed effects models. Fixed effects models grasp features of the municipality that are considered fixed (municipality-specific) and, as such, features that are not easily to alter in the short run (e.g. the availability of hospitals or health education programs).

There are two caveats. First, regional fixed effects models also controls for regional variation in the wage rate, and, consequently, the (attractiveness of the) LSH industry within that region compared to other sectors. Note, however, owing to the public nature of the LSH sector, large differences in wages between municipalities are not expected. Second, institutions and courses can have an influence on the development of general and specific skills. As such, instead of regional fixed effects models, one could also estimate course or educational institution fixed effects models in order to further control for unobserved individual and course characteristics (e.g. peer effects). We do not estimate these fixed effects models, however, because of data limitations. If one would estimate an institution or course fixed effects model, the total number of observations within each cluster, given our data set, would be too limited in order to estimate any significant results.

Multivariate regressions

After having performed iterative one-to-one matching, the multivariate regression estimates the difference in wages between comparable, homogenous workers in the different industries. We now construct a weighted standardized index of requested job-related general skills r_i by using principal components analysis (in Section 6, we show that, owing to rich data on job-related ability, index r_i is valid and reliable). We then may write:

$$y_i = cte + \beta I_i + \gamma r_i + \theta(I_i \times r_i) + \varepsilon_{mki},$$

if studied health profession =1. (7)

y_i denotes the log of hourly wages; I_i the treatment indicator; r_i requested job-related general skills; ($I_i \times r_i$) the interaction between the treatment indicator and requested job-related general skills; and ε_{mki} the error term. Note that regional fixed effects models are clustering the standard error at the level of m_k. The estimate of θ denotes the wage differential. θ captures the variance in wages that cannot be explained by differences in own or requested job-related general skills. We control for requested job-related general skills, so that positive differences in wages are not attributable to asking more skills (or productivity), but, instead, are the result of weighting the same skills differently.

6. Data

We use repeated cross section data of the Dutch higher vocational school leaving monitor (HBO) over the period 2003 to 2011. The data consist of (1) individual characteristics and job-related (cap)abilities of individuals; (2) educational features as type of education, educational program, field of education, and level of education; and (3) job characteristics as hourly wages, job hours, job search, field of the job, level of the job, skill use and skills short to perform in the job, and self-reported job match.

One year after graduation, all respondents were sent the school-leaving questionnaire (roa.unimaas.nl/hbomonitor). Every year about 600 graduates (10 percent) in nursing participated, so that we have (N=5,157) individuals in our sample in total. We observe that 14.66 percent of graduates (N=756) in the field of nursing dropped out of LSH only one year after graduation. From these 'dropouts', 114 (15.08 percent) are male, and 642 (84.92 percent) are female. In total, 617 male nurses are observed in the data, and 4,540 female nurses. As such, relatively, more males (18.48 percent) than females (14.14 percent) are leaving LSH one year after graduation.

Table 5 presents the industries in which the switchers are employed. The industries are categorized by using the international standard classification of occupations (ISCO). We observe that 37.35 percent of individuals with nursing credentials are employed in social science and related professions; 14.19 percent in personal care; and 6.43 percent in social work. These professions are to some extent related to professions in LSH, so that we classify these individuals' switch as horizontal mobility. However, we also track nurses in many different kinds of occupations, such as architects, engineers and rela ted professionals (3.48 percent); corporate managers (1.34 percent); physical and engineering science technicians (1.74 percent); and shop, stall and market salespersons (0.67 percent). Here, we classify these individuals' switch as vertical mobility. In order to control for 'horizontal and vertical industry mobility' in the multivariate regressions in Section 8, we create a dummy variable. The value of one indicates being employed in social sciences, social work or personal care; and the value of 0 otherwise.

		Freq.	Perc.			Freq.	Perc.
1	armed forces	2	0.27	26	administrative associate professionals	16	2.14
2	legislators, senior officials and managers	2	0.27	27	social work associate professionals	48	6.43
3	legislators and senior government officials	1	0.13	28	secretaries and keyboard-operating clerks	1	0.13
4	corporate managers	10	1.34	29	numerical clerks	3	0.4
5	production and operations managers	13	1.74	30	material-recording and transport clerks	5	0.67
6	managers of small enterprises	2	0.27	31	library, mail and related clerks	1	0.13
7	professionals	59	7.9	32	other office clerks	2	0.27
8	computing professionals	4	0.54	33	cashiers, tellers and related clerks	2	0.27
9	architects, engineers and related professionals	26	3.48	34	client information clerks	5	0.67
10	teaching professionals	2	0.27	35	travel attendants and related workers	1	0.13
11	secondary education teaching profession	19	2.54	36	housekeeping and restaurant services workers	2	0.27
12	primary and pre-primary education teacher	15	2.01	37	personal care and related workers	106	14.19
13	special education teaching professional	3	0.4	38	other personal services workers	1	0.13
14	other teaching professionals	2	0.27	39	protective services workers	4	0.54
15	business professionals	17	2.28	40	shop, stall and market salespersons	5	0.67
16	legal professionals	1	0.13	41	fishery workers, hunters and trappers	1	0.13
17	social science and related professional	279	37.35	42	machinery mechanics and fitters	1	0.13
18	writers and creative or performing artists	2	0.27	43	electrical and electronic equipment mechanics	1	0.13
19	public service administrative professionals	1	0.13	44	assemblers	1	0.13
20	technicians and associate professionals	14	1.87	45	motor vehicle drivers	1	0.13
21	physical and engineering science technicians	13	1.74	46	domestic and related helpers, cleaners	3	0.4
22	computer associate professionals	3	0.4	47	manufacturing laborers	1	0.13
23	optical and electronic equipment operators	37	4.95				
24	safety and quality inspectors	1	0.13				
25	finance and sales associate professionals	8	1.07				
					Total	747	100

Table 6-1 Industries in which the switchers are employed

7. Descriptive statistics

Table 6 summarizes the descriptive statistics of the variables: (1) hourly wages and log of hourly wages; (2) individual characteristics (i.e. age, gender, ethnicity and province of employment); (3) study program information (i.e. internship, and type of education); and (4) the questions with respect to own ability and requested ability for the job. We report the total number of observations, the mean values and differences between the mean values of the control group and the treatment group. The final column presents the T-values of an independent sample T-test.

The wages of nurses in the Netherlands is equal to about 15.32 euros per hour. This corresponds to the wages observed in the official Dutch statistics (loonwijzer.nl, 2014). In order to account for potential differences in working conditions between LSH-stayers and LSH-leavers, we choose not to work with gross monthly wages, but, instead, with hourly wage rates. Table 2 also summarizes descriptive statistics with respect to the log of hourly wages. We take the logarithm of wages, as to account for the parametric assumptions underlying multivariate regressions (see Section 5). We observe that, without controlling for covariates or following matching procedures, nurses who switch to other industries than LSH earn significantly +3 percent more than stayers.

Next, consider the individual characteristics of our sample. Overall, we observe only minor differences between treated and untreated individuals with respect to their characteristics. Only with respect to the type of study program, we observe significant mean differences between treated and untreated individuals. For instance, in the control group, there are significant fewer individuals who studied in part-time programs, and significant more individuals who studied in full-time and dual programs. And, on average, untreated individuals are about three years older than treated individuals.

	Mean Tg	Std Dev Tg	Mean Cg	Std Dev Cg	Diff Tg-Cg	T-value
Outcome						
Hourly wage (euros)	15.32	4.81	14.75	4.64	-0.57	-3.1
Hourly wage (log)	2.685	0.2962	2.6522	0.2722	-0.0327	-3
Individual characteristics						
age	30.22	9.35	27.72	8.04	2.5	7.7
gender (male=1)	0.1508	0.3581	0.1143	0.3182	0.037	2.9
non-Western migrant	0.0582	0.2343	0.045	0.2073	0.013	1.6
Western migrant	0.0265	0.1606	0.0275	0.1635	-0.001	-0.2
not a migrant	0.9153	0.2786	0.9275	0.2593	-0.012	-1.2
Study program information						
full time program	0.5304	0.4994	0.6128	0.4872	-0.082	-4.3
part time program	0.2804	0.4495	0.1347	0.3415	0.146	10.3
dual program	0.1892	0.3919	0.2524	0.4345	-0.063	-3.8
internship(yes=1)	0.9496	0.2189	0.9749	0.1563	-0.025	-3.9
Job province						
Groningen	0.0694	0.2544	0.0595	0.2365	0.01	1.1
Friesland	0.0592	0.2362	0.0541	0.2263	0.005	0.6
Drenthe	0.0347	0.183	0.0234	0.1511	0.011	1.9
Overijssel	0.0551	0.2283	0.0674	0.2507	-0.012	-1.3
Gelderland	0.1212	0.3266	0.1231	0.3286	-0.002	0.2
Utrecht	0.077	0.2668	0.1047	0.3062	-0.028	-2.4
Noord-Holland	0.1251	0.3311	0.1145	0.3184	0.011	0.9
Zuid-Holland	0.2237	0.417	0.2191	0.4137	0.005	0.3
Zeeland	0.0139	0.117	0.0159	0.1249	-0.002	-0.4
Noord-Brabant	0.157	0.364	0.147	0.3541	0.01	0.7
Limburg	0.0509	0.22	0.0606	0.2387	-0.01	-1.1
Flevoland	0.0128	0.1124	0.0108	0.1033	0.002	0.5

Table 6-2 Descriptive statistics of the treated (N=756) and untreated individuals (N=4401) with respect to individual and program characteristics (before matching)

	Mean Tg	Std Dev Tg	Mean Cg	Std Dev Cg	Diff Tg-Cg	T-value
own abilities (scale 1 to 5): ability to…						
apply field-specific knowledge in practice	3.78	0.67	3.86	0.64	-0.09	-3.39
use ICT	3.69	0.74	3.71	0.77	-0.02	-0.81
communicate in foreign languages	2.85	1.06	2.9	1.02	-0.05	-1.22
gather information	3.98	0.64	3.99	0.62	-0.01	-0.32
recognize problems and opportunities	3.99	0.63	3.99	0.61	0	0.07
draw connections	4.01	0.63	3.99	0.62	0.03	1.04
distinguish main priorities from side issues	3.91	0.63	3.92	0.62	0	-0.18
reason logically	4.04	0.62	4.05	0.61	-0.01	-0.33
work within budget/plan/guideline	3.63	0.81	3.56	0.82	0.07	2.23
work well under pressure	4.04	0.71	4.07	0.69	-0.03	-1.26
take decisive action	3.85	0.72	3.79	0.73	0.06	2.08
come up with new ideas and solutions	3.93	0.69	3.83	0.69	0.1	3.55
learn new things	4.17	0.66	4.19	0.62	-0.01	-0.52
make meaning clear to others	3.98	0.67	4.04	0.67	-0.06	-2.21
cooperate productively with others	4.15	0.64	4.25	0.61	-0.1	-4.06
mobilize the capacities of others	3.78	0.69	3.7	0.73	0.08	2.93
perform your work without supervision	4.32	0.63	4.27	0.64	0.06	2.28
requested abilities (scale 1 to 5)						
apply field-specific knowledge in practice	3.71	0.94	4.01	0.79	-0.3	-9.48
use ICT	3.43	0.96	3.43	0.95	0	0.04
communicate in foreign languages	2.03	1.06	2.26	1.04	-0.23	-5.69
gather information	3.76	0.92	3.85	0.83	-0.08	-2.56
recognize problems and opportunities	4.06	0.83	4.14	0.75	-0.08	-2.84
draw connections	4.01	0.86	4.18	0.73	-0.17	-5.88
distinguish main priorities from side issues	3.94	0.78	4.04	0.71	-0.11	-3.8
reason logically	3.97	0.8	4.08	0.71	-0.11	-4.01
work within budget/plan/guideline	3.56	1.06	3.55	1	0	0.08
work well under pressure	4.1	0.86	4.3	0.75	-0.2	-6.69
take decisive action	3.88	0.89	3.91	0.82	-0.03	-1.07
come up with new ideas and solutions	3.86	0.9	3.84	0.84	0.01	0.38
learn new things	3.84	0.92	3.99	0.84	-0.15	-4.47
make meaning clear to others	4.14	0.8	4.17	0.71	-0.03	-1.15
cooperate productively with others	4.16	0.79	4.27	0.72	-0.12	-4.18
mobilize the capacities of others	3.85	0.84	3.93	0.78	-0.08	-2.75
perform your work without supervision	4.35	0.72	4.36	0.69	-0.01	-0.41

Table 6-3 Descriptive statistics of the control group (Cg) and the treatment group (Tg) with respect to own and requested abilities (before matching)

Table 7 summarizes the descriptive statistics of own and requested job-related abilities. With respect to own job-related abilities, 7 out of 17 items have significant T-values (5 percent level), namely: (1) the ability to apply field-specific knowledge in practice (t=-3.39); (2) the ability to take decisive action (t=-2.08); (3) the ability to come up with new ideas and solutions (t=3.55); (4) the ability to make meaning clear to others (t=-2.21); (5) the ability to cooperate productively with others (t=-4.06); (6) the ability to mobilize the capacities of others (t=2.93); (7 the ability to perform your work without supervision (t=2.28). Note that the differences between the treatment group and the control group are always rather small.

Not surprisingly, we find 11 out of 17 items with respect to requested job-related abilities to be significantly different between the control group and the treatment group (see Table 7). Requested abilities to perform well in the job significantly differ between employment in LSH and foreign sectors. The highest mean difference between the control group and the treatment group is observed with respect to the question: ability to apply field-specific knowledge in practice (t=-9.48).

Based on the variables of Table 7, we construct two measures of ability, namely: (1) own job-related general skills; and (2) requested job-related general skills. Therefore, we use principal component analysis in order to reduce the dimension of having 17 items measuring ability into only 1 variable. Note that we have standardized the items, and only retain the first component constructed by the factor analysis. The own job-related general skills measure has an eigenvalue of 6.2169 (ρ=0.3657); the average inter-item correlation is 0.3077; and the scale reliability coefficient Cronbach's alpha is equal to 0.8831. The requested job-related general skills measure has an eigenvalue of 7.5401 (ρ=0.4436); the average inter-item correlation is 0.3893; and the scale reliability coefficient Cronbach's alpha is equal to 0.9155. From these statistics, we conclude that the own job-related general skills measure as well as the requested job-related general skills measure are valid and reliable.

8. Results

Matching results

In the first instance, we estimate the likelihood of a nurse to be in LSH employment conditional on his/her own job-related abilities by a discrete choice model (probit). Note that the responses on the ability questions were standardized before estimating the probit model. The results of the probit model are available upon request.

The results indicate that, on the one hand, individuals are likely to stay in LSH, if they are able to: apply field-specific knowledge into practice; work well under pressure; make meaning clear to others; and cooperate productively with others. On the other hand, they are more likely to switch, if they are able to work within budget/plan/guideline; come up with new ideas and solutions; mobilize the capacities of others; and perform your work without supervision.

As follows, we check whether the matching made `stayers' and `leavers' comparable with respect to their job-related abilities. Recall that we have matched treated individuals to untreated individuals based on own job-related ability.

Figure 2 and Figure 3 plot the distribution of both ability measures by employment in LSH (dotted line) or F (solid line), after iterative one-to-one matching. The Kolmogorov Smirnov test shows that own job-related general skills is equally distributed between sectors (KS=0.0296; P=0.468). This is desirable, as it shows that the matching worked. Not unexpectedly, we find an unequal distribution of requested job-related general skills between LSH and F (KS=0.1037; P=0.0000). Overall, the F industry requires less productivity from workers than LSH. However, this distributional difference between F and LSH is very small.

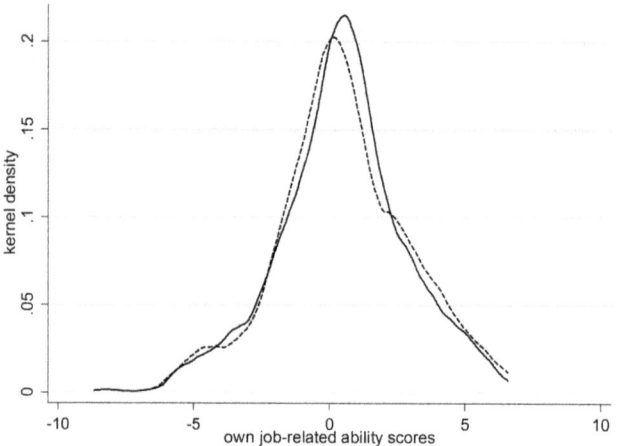

Figure 6-1 Kernel density of own ability scores by LHS employment (dotted line); and foreign industries (solid line). (Note: The Kolmogorov-Smirnov test points to equal distributions (chi=0.0424; P-value=0.506)

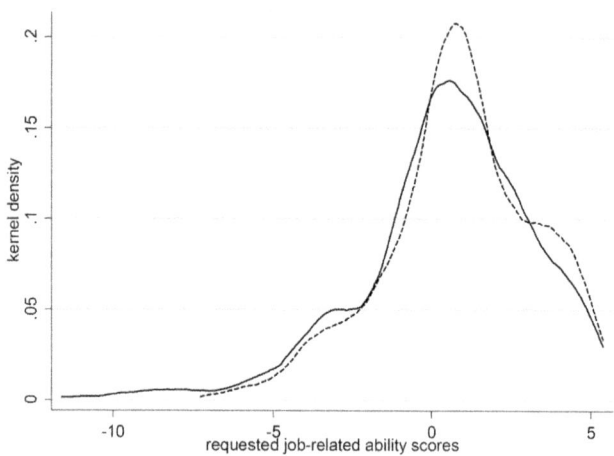

Figure 6-2 Kernel density of requested ability scores by LHS employment (dotted line); and foreign sectors (solid line). (Note: The Kolmogorov-Smirnov test points to unequal distributions (chi=0.0849; P-value=0.009)

Estimated wage differentials

The main results are summarized in Table 8. We present four subsequent models, namely: (1) wage differentials estimated by pooled ordinary least squares (pooled OLS[8]) without iterative one-to-one matching in Model 1; (2) wage differentials estimated by iterative one-to-one matching in Model 2; (3) wage differentials estimated for female nurses only; and (4) wage differentials estimated for female nurses only and controlled for seniority. Robust standard errors are presented between brackets. Each model is estimated by using regional fixed effects.

	Model 1		Model 2		Model 3		Model 4	
Employment (F=1)	0.0311	**	0.0129		0.0038		-0.0163	
	(0.0149)		(0.0210)		(0.0226)		(0.0181)	
Requested ability	0.0029		0.0039		0.0004		0.0034	
	(0.0022)		(0.0047)		(0.0052)		(0.0037)	
Wage differential	0.0208	***	0.0214	***	0.0248	***	0.0164	***
	(0.0053)		(0.0073)		(0.0073)		(0.0060)	
Matching variables	-		Own abilities		Own abilities		Own abilities	
Control variables	None		None		Gender		Gender Seniority	
Specification	OLS		NNM		NNM		NNM	
Caliper			0.01		0.01		0.01	
Std.error	Cl(jcity)		Cl(jcity)		Cl(jcity)		Cl(jcity)	
	321		237		226		226	
Obs.	5,157		1,508		1,307 (Only women)		1,307 (Only women)	

Note: NNM denotes Nearest Neighbor Matching

Table 6-4 Summary of estimation output (outcome variable = log wages)

---

[8] Note that the OLS estimates are pooled over the years 2003-2011.

First, consider briefly the results of the estimate of β. The estimate of $β_1$ is equal to +3.11 percent significant at 5 percent level in Model 1. This estimate drops to insignificant values once appropriately accounted for job-related ability in the other three models. Consider also the association between job-requested ability and log wages. We find that the estimate of $γ$ is not significant and equal to +0.29 percent in Model 1. This finding is unchanged in the other models.

The estimate of interest is the inter-industry wage differential, namely parameter θ. In Model 1, the wage differential (θ=+2.08 percent) is significant at 1 percent level. Controlling for underlying differences with respect to job-related skills in the population between 'stayers' and 'switchers', the wage differential is equal to (θ=+2.14 percent) significant at 1 percent level in Model 2.

Next, we estimate the multivariate regression separately by gender. Therefore, we first drop the male nurses from the data, so that only female nurses are included in the multivariate regression. These results are visualized in Table 8, Model 3. The results for keeping only the male nurses are available upon request. For female nurses, the estimated wage differential θ is equal to +2.48 percent significant at 1 percent level in Model 4. For male nurses, the estimated wage differential θ is +1.21 percent and not significant. From this we may conclude that the wage differential, as estimated in the previous Model 2, is mainly driven by female nurses. However, note that owing to the small sample size of male nurses, this finding can be subject to a type-II statistical error, so that we may falsely accept the null hypothesis of no significant wage differential.

In Model 4, we additionally control for seniority by including the variable age in the multivariate regression.[9] The estimated wage differential θ for female nurses drops to +1.51 percent, however, remains significant at 5 percent level. As such, seniority partially explains wage differences between stayers and leavers.

Industry mobility and non-monetary aspects of the nursing job

The results of the robustness checks are summarized in Table 9. Full model estimation output is available upon request. We provide four robustness checks in total for θ, the estimated wage differential.

First, we control for gender, ethnicity, and study program information in Model 5. The influence of the variables `internship`, `part-time program`, and `dual program` on θ may be particularly interesting. Geel et al. (2011) discuss that employers bear an increasing share of education and training costs the more specific the skills workers have to learn. As a result, apprenticeship training, for instance by internships, dual tracks or part-time programs, goes along with workers' occupational immobility (Geel et al., 2011). However, controlling for these variables does not capture the estimated wage differential (θ=+1.44 percent). These results are in line with Model 4 from Table 8.

Second, we classify individuals' switch as 'vertical' or 'horizontal' inter-industry mobility. It is in this respect that McGuinness and Sloane (2009) show substantial wage penalties for `over-education`, for men and women, and for `over-skilling`, for men only. In Model 6, we drop the data of all individuals who switched vertically, and then compare horizontally switchers to stayers. This is in contrast to Model 7, where we drop the data

---

[9] The estimate of age indicates that a one-year increase in age is associated with +1.65 percent higher wages.

of all individuals who switched horizontally, and then compare vertically switchers to stayers. The results indicate that vertical mobility drives the estimated wage differential, as θ is not significantly different from zero in Model 6, whereas θ is equal to +2.14 percent significant at 5 percent level in Model 7.

	Model 5	Model 6	Model 7	Model 8
Employment (F=1)	-0.0211	0.0005	-0.0345	-0.03246
	(0.0163)	(0.0164)	(0.0299)	(0.0380)
Requested ability	0.0045	0.0065	0.0029	0.0003
	(0.0033)	(0.0036)	(0.0085)	(0.0086)
Wage differential	0.0144 **	0.0065	0.0214 **	0.0236 **
	(0.0056)	(0.0061)	(0.0118)	(0.0121)
Matching variables	Own abilities	Own abilities	Own abilities	Own abilities
Control variables	Seniority Characteristics Study program	Seniority Characteristics Study program Horizontal mobility	Seniority Characteristics Study program - Vertical mobility	Seniority Characteristics Study program - Vertical mobility Non-monetary
Specification	NNM	NNM	NNM	NNM
Caliper	0.01	0.01	0.01	0.01
Std.error	Cl(jcity) 237	Cl(jcity) 213	Cl(jcity) 167	Cl(jcity) 155
Obs.	1,508	1,185	643	565

Note: NNM denotes Nearest Neighbor Matching.

Table 6-5 Summary of robustness checks (outcome variable = log wages)

To conclude, in line with the critiques from Di Tommaso et al. (2009), we control for several other than monetary aspects of the job, namely: (1) type of contract; (2) the size of the organization wherein the individual works; (3) tasks of supervision; (4) whether the job has good career opportunities; (5) satisfaction with current work; and (6) information on the level of job (mis-)match. The estimate of θ is still significant and equal to +2.36 percent significant at 5 percent level in Model 8.

9. Discussion and conclusions

This chapter contributes to the previous literature on inter-industry wage differentials and job-related ability. We apply the skill-weights approach of Lazaer (2009) on the potential switch graduates in nursing can make from the life sciences and health industry to other, foreign industries, and estimate its effect on wages. The skill-weights approach argues that nurses will voluntary leave the LSH industry for a job outside LSH, in case seniority in LSH is lower than the returns to weighted general skills in other, foreign industries. The empirical strategy benefits from unique data on job-related general skills. These skills are the direct result of innate ability and individuals' background characteristics, on the one hand, and education in school and experience on-the-job, on the other hand. Owing to iterative one-to-one matching, we make graduates homogenous with respect to their background characteristics and abilities. The empirical strategy also deals with regional variation in employment opportunities in LSH.

The results from the estimated wage differentials are in line with the model predictions of Lazaer (2009): nurses who quit LSH earn, on average, higher (+2.14 percent) wages in other, foreign industries. Seniority can partially explain the estimated wage differential. The effect size is small, but can be supported by the elasticity of labor supply of nurses (Phillips, 1995; Askildsen et al., 2003; Shields, 2004; Di Tommaso et al., 2009). These results are driven by female nurses and by vertical industry mobility (i.e. `true' foreign industries), not by horizontal industry mobility. Non-monetary aspects of the nursing job do not capture the effect, so that we can conclude that our estimated inter-industry wage differential is robust to several model specifications and control variables.

This chapter also provides valuable insights into the rise of recruitment bottlenecks in LSH by using the concept of market thickness. In general, risk-averse people will have the propensity to obtain a diploma that put high weights on learning skills vital for employment in the `thick markets'. In knowledge societies, such as the Netherlands, thick markets arise for skill-intensive jobs, and recruitment bottlenecks are heavily associated with low end (industry-specific) vocational education or training (for a policy discussion on skill utilization in EU-27, see cedefop.europa.eu). The LSH industry behaves as a rather thin market. Studying health and welfare education or training largely involves the acquisition of industry-specific skills, and, to lesser extent, the acquisition of general skills (Hirsch and Schumacher, 2012). As individuals with nursing credentials cannot, or only to limited extent, apply their industry-specific skills in other than LSH industries, the potential switch a nurse can make directly implies the loss of suitability of industry-specific skills, and, consequently, the loss of investment in industry-specific education and training. The study, therefore, can be considered hazardous for people who are uncertain about the discounted value of health and welfare education or training.

Our findings, embedded in the skill-weights approach, also argue the chronic nature of recruitment bottlenecks in LSH. Seniority and skills' payoff are embedded in the industry structure, and, therefore, not easily to alter in the short run. The policy discussion in this respect is twofold: on the one hand, nurses are underpaid and unions are fighting for wage increase (for a discussion, see also Taylor, 2007). On the other hand, health care costs are rising and policymakers wish to cut costs also through freezing, or even lowering wages of health professionals. The LSH industry may well find its solution in the demand for informal care. Dutch policymakers already discuss the evolution from a `welfare state' to a `participation society', a society wherein every individual takes up its responsibility in caring for sick or senior family members or friends in order to cut in health care costs (King Willem-Alexander's speech from the throne, Prinsjesdag September 17th 2013, see rijksoverheid.nl). However, it is in this respect that Heitmueller and Inglis (2007) discuss substantial wage losses of informal care givers as a result of non-labor market participation.

Further research particularly dealing with horizontal industry mobility should focus on the extent to which nurses, who left the LSH industry, have an option to return to nursing. For instance, young graduates might need a few years to decide what the best occupation for them is. It should also focus on the decision to study health and welfare education or training in order to better understand the discrepancy between the perceived and actual discounted value of health and welfare education or training.

References

Askildsen, J., Baltagi, B. and Holmås, T. (2003). Will increased wages reduce shortages of nurses? A panel data analysis of nurses' labor supply. Health Economics 12, 705--719.

Acemoglu, D. (2001) Good jobs versus bad jobs. Journal of Labor Economics 19(1), 1-21.

Booton, L.A. and Lane, J.I. (1985) Hospital market structure and the return to nursing education. Journal of Human Resources 20(2), 184-196.

Botelho, A., Jones, C.B. and Kiker, B.F. (1998) Nursing wages and educational credentials: the role of work experience and selectivity bias. Economics of Education Review 17(3), 297-306.

Cabus, S.J. and Haelermans, C. (2013). Work or Schooling? On The Return to Gaining in-School Work Experiences. TIER working paper 13/11.

CBS (2012) Gezondheidszorg in cijfers. Centraal Planbureau voor de Statistiek. Den Haag/Heerlen.

Cedefop (2012). Europe's skill challenge. Lagging skill demand increases risks of skill mismatch. Briefing note Match 2012, ISNN 1831-2411.

Dickens, W.T. and Katz, L.F. (1987) Inter-industry wage differences and theories of wage determination. NBER Working Paper 2271.

Di Tommaso, M.L., Strøm, S. and Sæther, E.M. (2009) Nurses wanted Is the job too harsh or is the wage too low? Journal of Health Economics 28(3), 748-757.

Dustmann, C. and Pereira, S.C. (2008).Wage growth and job mobility in the United Kingdom and Germany. Industrial and Labor Relations Review 61(3), 374-393.

Elliot, R.F., Ma, A.H.Y., Scott, A., Bell, D. and Roberts, E. (2007). Geographically differentiated pay in the labour market for nurses. Journal of Health Economics 26, 190-212.

Fishe, R.P.H., Trost, R.P. and Lurie, P.M. (1981) Labor force earnings and college choice of young women: an examination of selectivity bias and comparative advantage. Economics of Education Review 1(2), 169-191.

Gautier, P.A., Teulings, C.N. and Vuuren, van, A. (2010) On-the-job search, mismatch and efficiency. Review of Economic Studies 77, 245-272.

Geel, R., Mure, J., Backes-Gellner, U. (2011). Specificity of occupational training and occupational mobility: an empirical study based on Lazear's skill-weights approach. Education Economics 19(5), 519-535.

Gibbons, R. and Katz, L. (1992) Does unmeasured ability explain inter-industry wage differentials? Review of Economic Studies 59, 515-535.

Gill, A.M. and Leigh, D.E. (2001) Do the returns to community college differ between academic and vocational programs? Journal of Human Resources 38(1), 134-155.

Groshen, E.L. (1991) The structure of the female/male wage differential: is it who you are, what you do, or where you work? Journal of Human Resources 26(3), 457-472.

Handy, F. and Katz, E. (1998) The wage differential between nonprofit institutions and corporations: getting more pay less? Journal of Comparative Economics 26, 246-261.

Hanushek, E. A., Woessman, L., and Zhang, L. (2011). General Education, Vocational Education, and Labor-Market Outcomes over the Life-Cycle. NBER Working Paper 17504.

Heitmueller, A. and Inglis, K. (2007) The earnings of informal carers: Wage differentials and opportunity costs. Journal of Health Economics 26(4), 821--841.

Heywood, J.S. and Halloran, P.L. (2005) Racial earnings differentials and performance pay. Journal of Human Resources XL, 435-452.

Heywood, J.S. and Parent D. (2012) Performance pay and the White-Black gap. Journal of Labor Economics 30(2), 249-290.

Hirsch, B.T. and Schumacher, E.J. (2012) Underpaid or Overpaid? Wage Analysis for Nurses Using Job and Worker Attributes. Southern Economic Journal 78(4), 1096-1119.

Hurd, R.W. (1973) Equilibrium vacancies in a labor market dominated by non-profit firms: the "shortage" of nurses. Review of Economics and Statistics 55(2), 234-240.

Johnson, W.G. and Lambrinos, J. (1985) Wage discrimination against handicapped men and women. Journal of Human Resources 20(2), 264-277.

Jones, C.B. and Gates, M. (2004) Gender-based wage differentials in a predominantly female profession: observations from nursing. Economics of Education Review 23, 615-631.

Kevätsalo, K. (2007). Internet as a trade union tool. – WageIndicator and Finnish nurses as an example. Publication Series B: Surveys 4/2007, 30.

Kidd, M.P., Sloane, P.J. and Ferko, I. (2000) Disability and the labour market: an analysis of British males. Journal of Health Economics 19, 961-981.

Krueger, A. and Summers, L.H. (1986) Reflections on the inter-industry wage structure. NBER Working Paper 1968.

Krueger, A. and Summers, L.H. (1988) Efficiency wages and the inter-undustry wage structure. Econometrica 56(2), 259-293.

Lam, K-C. and Liu, P-W. Earnings divergence of immigrants. Journal of Labor Economics 20(1), 86-104.

Lazaer, E.P. (2009). Firm-specific human capital: a skill-weights approach. Journal of Political Economy 117(5), 914-940.

Link, C.R. (1988) Returns to nursing education: 1970-84. Journal of Human Resources 23(3), 372-387.

Maestad, O., Torsvik, G. and Aakvik, A. (2010). Overworked? On the relationship between workload and health worker performance. Journal of Health Economics 29(5), 686-698.

McGuinness, S. and Sloane, P. (2009) Labour market mismatch among UK graduates: an analysis using REFLEX data. IZA Discussion Paper 4168, 49.

Melly, B. (2005) Public-private industry wage differentials in Germany: evidence from quantile regression. Empirical Economics 30, 505-520.

Pissadires, C.A. (1994) Search unemployment with on-the-job search. Review of Economic Studies 61(3), 457-475.

Roy, A. (1951) Some thoughts on the distribution of earnings. Oxford Economic Papers 3, 135-146.

Spence, M. (1973). Job Market Signaling. The Quarterly Journal of Economics 87(3), 355-374.

Shields, M.A. (2004). Addressing nurse shortages: what can policy makers learn from the econometric evidence of nurse labor supply. The Economic Journal 114, F464--F498.

Shields, M.A. and Ward, M. (2001). Improving nurse retention in the National Health Service in England: the impact of job satisfaction on intentions to quit. Journal of Health Economics 20, 677--701.

Phillips, V.L. (1995). Nurses' labor supply: participation, hours of work, and discontinuities in the supply function. Journal of Health Economics 14, 567--582.

Taylor, L.J. (2007). Optimal wages in the market for nurses: An analysis based on Heyes' model. Journal of Health Economics 27, 1027--1030.

World Health Organization (2011). Global Health and Ageing. NIH Publication 11-7737, National Institute on Ageing, National Institute of Health, U.S. Department of Health and Human Services, 32.

Yett, D. (1966). The nursing shortage and the Nurse Training Act of 1964. Industrial and Labor Relations Review 19(2), 190-200.

Yildirim, D. and Aycan, Z. (2008). Nurses' work demands and work--family conflict: A questionnaire survey. International Journal of Nursing Studies 45(9), 1366--1378.

Short Author Bios of the Corresponding Authors

Kristof De Witte (Editor)

Kristof De Witte is an associate professor at the research center 'Leuven Economics of Education Research' at KU Leuven, Belgium, and at Top Institute for Evidence Based Education Research (TIER) at Maastricht University, the Netherlands. He is also a guest researcher at Amsterdam School of Economics. At Maastricht University, he is chairman of the Program Committee of the MEBIT post-initial program for teachers. At KU Leuven he coordinates the higher secondary teacher training program (SLO Economie) in economics and the research group 'Leuven Economics of Education Research'. Leuven Economics of Education Research (LEER), is a research and education center of the Faculty of Economics and Business. It aims for state-of-the-art academic research on education and education-labour market issues with economic tools. He is detached to the Dutch Ministry of Education as an expert for the 'Review Commission Dutch Higher Education and Research'.

The research interests of Kristof De Witte comprise education economics, performance evaluation and early school leaving. He published his work in many international academic journals and has various publications in Dutch field and policy journals. He is a member of the international advisory board of 'International Journal of Productivity Management and Assessment Technology' and external reviewer for the Dutch testing institute CITO. Dr. De Witte received two international prizes for his doctoral dissertation, a paper prize, an award for his undergraduate thesis, and an award at the end of secondary education. He spent more than 9 months abroad in academic visits at, among others, Columbia University and Aston University. His Google Scholar citation page counts more than 750 citations, a h-index of 17 and an i10-index of 24.

Tommaso Agasisti

My research activity is focused on Public Finance and Management, and the mainstream is in the field of economics of education. I work on financing models for higher education systems, both from empirical and theoretical perspectives. Moreover, my studies deal with the efficiency analysis of educational institutions, especially in higher education. Lastly, my researches are also about the management of universities, within the framework of new public management. Recently, I also started working on school choice and the analysis of educational production functions and efficiency. My research papers are published in academic journals such as Economics Letters, Applied Economics, International Review of Applied Economics, Education Economics, Higher Education, Higher Education Quarterly, Journal of Higher Education Policy and Management, Tertiary Education and Management. I am referee for academic journals, many of which listed in the ISI Social Science Index: Education Economics (EE), Higher Education (HighEd), Educational Evaluation and Policy Analysis (EEPA), Evaluation and Program Planning (EPP), Minerva, Asia Pacific Education Review (APER), Operational Research: An International Journal (ORIJ), Studies in Educational Evaluation, Hacienda Pública Española. I wrote several book reviews for the journal Education Economics. I also served as consultant for the Economics Area – Routledge Editor (Taylor & Francis Group).

Jos Blank

Jos Blank is an associate professor in Public Sector Efficiency at Delft University of Technology. He is the founder of the centre for Innovation and Public Sector Efficiency (IPSE-Studies), which carries out research on the efficiency and the effectiveness of the public sector. IPSE Studies not only aims at academic research, but also at contributing to the policy discussions concerning the optimal design of the public sector. The latter also includes the implementation of research results in everyday policy.

Jos has 20 years of experience in public sector efficiency research. He wrote many (national and international) articles and some books about the productivity of the public services in the Netherlands. Most of his work relates to the health care and education sector. More specifically, Jos has worked on, among other things, the structure of costs in nursing homes, hospitals, institutes for the mentally disabled, primary and secondary schools and companies for provision of social employment. Also, Jos has been involved in efficiency research for the water industry and the police forces. At the moment, he is working at a research about bureaucracy in the education sector.

He is also an active member of the Productivity Analysis Research Network, has joined several official committees about benchmarking in the public sector, and is a referee for various different international journals. Previous employment positions of Jos were at Statistics Netherlands (CBS), the Social and Cultural Planning Office of the Netherlands (SCP) and ECORYS-NEI.

Chris van Klaveren

Chris Van Klaveren studied economics at the University of Amsterdam and graduated in 2002. During his study he worked as a consultant for The World Bank in 2001. In 2009 he obtained his PhD in Economics from the University of Amsterdam entitled "The Intra-household Allocation of Time". He is currently assistant professor at Maastricht University and University of Amsterdam.

Inge de Wolf

Inge de Wolf is professor at Maastricht University. She worked before as a program manager for the Dutch Education Inspectorate. Her research focusses on the quality of schools, the effects of inspection and 'what works in education'. She is affiliated with the Dutch Top Institute for Evidence Based Education Research.

Oliver Holz

Oliver Holz is an associated professor at the Specific Teacher Training department at the University of Leuven (campus Brussels) and a member of the research center 'Leuven Economics of Education Research'. He is Master in Educational Sciences, Psychology and Physical Education (Chemnitz; Germany); PhD in comparative education about the current situation of the compulsory education in Sweden with special attention on the integration of the European Dimension in the educational system; he is living in Belgium since 2003; he is participant in and coordinator of different European projects; he published his work in different publications and different languages.

Short Author Bios of the Corresponding Authors

Nick Deschacht

Nick Deschacht is lecturer at the Faculty of Economics and Business of KU Leuven (Brussels campus). He is a labour economist and holds a PhD in Applied Economics from the Vrije Universiteit Brussel. He currently teaches econometrics, statistics, research methods and international economics.

Katie Goeman

Katie Goeman holds a PhD in Social Sciences. In November 2009 she was appointed Project Leader for Educational Innovation at the faculty of Economics and Business of the KU Leuven (campus Brussels). She coordinates the introduction of innovations in higher education and lifelong learning settings, and is responsible for carrying out research projects involving the investigation of ICT/media applications for education and training purposes (course and curriculum design, persistence and performance, monitoring). To this end she is affiliated as a researcher with the Centre for Instructional Psychology and Technology at the faculty of Psychology and Pedagogical Sciences (KU Leuven).

Sofie Cabus

Sofie Cabus studied business management at HU Brussels in 2003-07 and public economics at KU Leuven (2007-08). In 2008-10, she worked for one year as a research associate at the Research Institute for Work and Society (HIVA-KU Leuven) and at the Center for Disability and Integration (CDI-USG). Dr. Cabus obtained her PhD in economics at Maastricht University (2010-13), and was a visiting scholar at Columbia University, Teachers College, in 2012. She currently works as an assistant professor at Maastricht University, and is affiliated with the Top Institute for Evidence Based Education Research (tierweb.nl) and the Dutch Teachers and Policy Makers Academy (dtpa.nl). Her research interests include the economics of education, health and labor economics, and modern applied microeconometric methods and techniques.

www.ingramcontent.com/pod-product-compliance
Ingram Content Group UK Ltd.
Pitfield, Milton Keynes, MK11 3LW, UK
UKHW021834140426
5217IPUK00021B/1447